MW01487259

Going Deeper
by David Hoffmeister
ISBN: 978-0-9884327-9-6

Copyright © 1994, 2013, 2016
Living Miracles Publications

Second Printed Edition 2016

Living Miracles Publications
P.O. Box 789, Kamas, UT 84036 USA
publishing@livingmiraclescenter.org
+1 435.200.4076

LIVING MIRACLES

This book was joyfully produced by the Living Miracles Community –
a non-profit ministry run by inspired mystics devoted to awakening.

# Going Deeper

Going Deeper – One Problem, One Solution
A Dialogue about Transcending
the Subject/Object Split

David Hoffmeister

## DAVID HOFFMEISTER

David Hoffmeister is a modern-day mystic who has traveled to over forty countries and forty-nine states to share the message of Love, Oneness and Freedom. He is a living demonstration that peace is possible. His gentle demeanor and articulate, non-compromising expression have touched lives everywhere and are a gift to all.

David's journey involved the study of many pathways culminating in a deeply committed practical application of A Course in Miracles. Through countless miracles David came to the realization that he could "step back and let Him lead the way." (W-155) Divine Providence is a practical reality that David teaches and experiences; it is the acceptance of complete dependence on God and surrender to trust in the Holy Spirit's plan.

> Nothing you need will be denied you. Not one seeming difficulty but will melt away before you reach it. You need take thought for nothing, careless of everything except the only purpose that you would fulfill. (T-20.IV.8)

David's life continues to be a living demonstration of the Awakened Mind. His teachings have been translated into 13 languages, and taken into the hearts and minds of millions through the intimate style of his books, audios, and videos. There are Centers devoted to his teachings in the USA, Mexico, Europe, Australia and Canada.

# TABLE OF CONTENTS

*A Course in Miracles*
Reference Abbreviations

T: Text
M: Manual for Teachers
W: Workbook for Students

# INTRODUCTION

The following dialogue goes deep into the practical application of workbook lesson 79 from *A Course in Miracles*. Specific thoughts, issues and questions are followed inward to the point of seeing that there are no problems outside the mind. Salvation is accomplished through the recognition that there is just one problem and one solution. We begin our dialogue by reading the lesson in its entirety.

## Lesson 79

Let me recognize the problem so it can be solved.

A problem cannot be solved if you do not know what it is. Even if it is really solved already you will still have the problem, because you will not recognize that it has been solved. This is the situation of the world. The problem of separation, which is really the only problem, has already been solved. Yet the solution is not recognized because the problem is not recognized.

Everyone in this world seems to have his own special problems. Yet they are all the same, and must be recognized as one if the one solution that solves them all is to be accepted. Who can see that a problem has been solved if he thinks the problem is something else? Even if he is given the answer, he cannot see its relevance.

That is the position in which you find yourself now. You have the answer, but you are still uncertain about what the problem is. A long series of different problems seems to confront you, and as one is settled the next one and the next arise. There seems to be no end to them. There is no time in which you feel completely free of problems and at peace.

The temptation to regard problems as many is the temptation to keep the problem of separation unsolved. The world seems to present you with a vast number of problems, each requiring a different answer. This perception places you in a position in which your problem solving must be inadequate, and failure is inevitable.

No one could solve all the problems the world appears to hold. They seem to be on so many levels, in such varying forms and with such varied content, that they confront you with an impossible situation. Dismay and depression are inevitable as you regard them. Some spring up unexpectedly, just as you think you have resolved the previous ones. Others remain unsolved under a cloud of denial, and rise to haunt you from time to time, only to be hidden again but still unsolved.

All this complexity is but a desperate attempt not to recognize the problem, and therefore not to let it be resolved. If you could recognize that your only problem is separation, no matter what form it takes, you could accept the answer because you would see its relevance. Perceiving the underlying constancy in all the problems that seem to confront you, you would understand that you have the means to solve them all. And you would use the means, because you recognize the problem.

In our longer practice periods today we will ask what the problem is, and what is the answer to it. We will not assume that we already know. We will try to free our minds of all the many different kinds of problems we think we have. We will try to realize that we have only one problem, which we have failed to recognize. We will ask what it is, and wait for the answer. We will be told. Then we will ask for the solution to it. And we will be told.

The exercises for today will be successful to the extent to which you do not insist on defining the problem. Perhaps you will not succeed in letting all your preconceived notions go, but that is not necessary. All that is necessary is to entertain some doubt about the reality of your version of what your problems are. You are trying to recognize that you have been given the answer by recognizing the problem, so that the problem and the answer can be brought together and you can be at peace.

The shorter practice periods for today will not be set by time, but by need. You will see many problems today, each one calling for an answer. Our efforts will be directed toward recognizing that there is only one problem and one answer. In this recognition are all problems resolved. In this recognition there is peace.

Be not deceived by the form of problems today. Whenever any difficulty seems to rise, tell yourself quickly:

Let me recognize this problem so it can be solved.

Then try to suspend all judgment about what the problem is. If possible, close your eyes for a moment and ask what it is. You will be heard and you will be answered. (W-79)

David: This is a good starting point. We can talk about personal issues or problems, such as feelings of anger or hatred or grievances. Perhaps we think there are medical problems, such as aches, pains, disease, or sickness, or other seeming problems with the body. We may think of talking more on a collective scale, for example social issues such as abortion or gay rights, etc. There seems to be a wide array of problems. We will bring each seeming problem back to the mind and redefine what we perceive it to be.

To begin let's take a look at what the mind is and how it is differentiated from the world of our senses – the world of change and constant fluctuation. We have the term "mind," but the mind is not contained in the world. The mind is not analogous to the brain. Mind is the activating agent of Spirit. It is very powerful; it is the place where the mechanism of decision-making is contained. It is abstract. There is no fitting metaphor or analogy for it in the world because the mind is not limited. Everything in the world that we see is limited or fragmented in some way.

We can take any particular issue or question and work it back using the framework that we have just set up. We will see that there is no problem outside the mind.

Friend: Last week I was in an environment that was much noisier and more active than I am used to. There is a thought that I need to be in a quiet external environment to have the internal experience of quiet. I still have the thought that my internal state of mind is dependent on external conditions such as the noise or level of activity going on around me.

David: OK. You perceive the problem as an issue with the environment; you perceive certain undesirable circumstances as outside you. When we bring it back to the metaphysics of the Course we see that one of the basic premises is that "there is nothing outside you." (T-18.VI.1) The inner world and the outer world are not different. They are actually one and the same – simultaneous. The belief that they are different sets up a situation or a conflict; *it would be more conducive for me if I were in a different situation or a different place.* Right away we see the belief that you are *in* a certain environment.

4

# Duality – Subject/Object Split

David: As we listen to the words we use, we see that they can be used as clues to what we really believe. First of all, the belief that one is *in* an environment points back to the belief that I am a person who is in the world and distinct from the world. There is a belief that I am a person who can act on the world and be acted upon by the world. This is the subject/object split. We have the personal "I" – I am a subject in the world and I subjectively perceive the world. I have emotions; I have likes and dislikes; I have the ability to make decisions as a person; I believe that others have the ability to make decisions as persons. The split between subject and object is the discomfort you feel in those situations where there seems to be activity and high noise levels. The problem as defined in the world seems to be that if it was quieter you could be at peace.

Friend: Yes. My mind would be more still than otherwise.

David: Your state of mind is dependent on the environment in this case. And to take it one step further, as we have just done, the environment is something that is not you. There is an environment that is apart from you that is being objectified. For example, the boys you are staying with seem to be part of the objectified environment in which you find yourself.

Friend: That is where the split comes in, between the inner and the outer in my mind.

David: It is a very basic split. It is a subject/object split; the subject is seen to be you – a person – and the object can be another person or an object.

Friend: Everything is seen outside of me, outside of what I perceive as me.

David: Right, everything is outside of what you perceive as you. There is a split and this split is in the mind. It is a choice; it is a way of perceiving that the mind has chosen. To fuse the split – to see no duality between oneself and the world – can seem to be a big leap. It can seem to be unfathomable, impossible even, as if there is no experiential grounding or basis for it. The first step in transcending that split – or letting it go in the mind – is to take a look at the dynamics of *why*. Why does the mind make that split? What purpose does it serve the mind to make a subject/object split?

Friend: I think duality is projected to relieve the pressure of the conflicting thought systems that the mind is trying to maintain within it. The mind tries to throw one thought system outside of itself in an attempt to ease the pressure and make it more manageable and less confronting. That is how the duality is set up. It is experienced as being outside of the mind instead of inside the mind, where it feels intolerable. There is a kind of pseudo-belief or misconception that placing it outside will relieve the conflict in the mind.

David: You say intolerable. As you go along, moment by moment, do you have a sense of the strength of this intolerance? Can you sense the force of it as you feel the pull towards defining the problem in the world? That is an indicator that there is a tremendous amount of fear behind that pull; there is something the mind is running from. The projecting game of blaming and defining problems as being in the world is perpetuated by this insistent avoidance.

Friend: Are you talking about the fear of God that is in the mind – the fear of punishment that is believed to be deserved for thinking that we really separated from God?

David: Yes, though that can seem very abstract. It is common for people to say that they are not in touch with that; they don't really see that they are afraid of God or afraid of love. But the problem you shared can be stated as: *I am not at peace and I could be at peace if something were different in my environment.* This is a good example of the core of what goes on in this world as a defense against making the metaphysical connection of coming to know that *there is only one problem and one solution.* This defense runs deep and is very persistent. It will continue to reoccur until we can really see what is going on. Whenever a situation arises that you want to be different than it is, just remember that you are having a perceptual problem.

Friend: I remember thinking that it could be a great opportunity to learn to get quiet no matter how active and noisy the environment is. I know that there is a way to be at peace *regardless*, but without experientially knowing what that feels like, it is just talk.

David: OK. Take that idea of experience versus talk; let's look at it in the context of this holy encounter right now. Are there unresolved problems, situations or uncomfortable thoughts that you are in touch with right now?

## TRACING IT BACK

Friend: Well, I feel self-conscious about recording this conversation. I want to completely ignore it and just be in dialogue with you but I am feeling self-conscious.

David: Let's explore that. You are feeling a sense of uneasiness about the recorder going. If you go into that, what is the uneasiness about?

Friend: Usually when we are in dialogue I am mostly just thinking about what we are talking about. I notice that with the microphone setup I am not nearly as attentive to what we are saying to each other.

David: If we look at that through the lens of the subject/object split that we are talking about, we see the belief that I am a person and that you are a person. We have had dialogues in the past that seemed to be quite focused, yet now the microphone and recording equipment are making something different.

Friend: Obviously there is something going on in my mind for me to think that it is different.

David: There are so many subtle ways in which the subject/object split can manifest itself in the sense that these are beliefs we are talking about. You really *believe* that it is different than it was. You believe that there is a different factor added on now. Attention gets distracted by that dynamic, away from our intention to come here and cut through things. Is there anything else to your feeling of being self-conscious? Is there a sense of censorship about what you say when it is being recorded as opposed to when it is not?

Friend: I am aware that it could be helpful to be as clear as possible when I am speaking. I guess I am trying to be more attentive to a kind of censoring of what I say and how I say it.

## BELIEFS AND ASSUMPTIONS

David: We are not consciously aware of everything that we believe. There is a belief system in operation and there are a lot of assumptions and premises that are tied into it. We can use this dialogue as an exploration of your belief system, as something that you can go back to – to hear yourself. You can use it like a mirror, to see things about yourself that you were not aware of, deepening your awareness. In that sense you can think of it as another tool.

Friend: I notice that it feels different to me if I think I am the only one that is going to hear this recording than if I think that this is something that is going to be shared with other people.

David: That's a good point; that really gets into the subject/object split and the self-concept. This is saying that there is a world outside your mind that is apart from the personhood of who you think you are. Your identity is tied in with other people that you call friends and acquaintances. The self-conscious thought is, *Other people may hear this. What will they think of me? Are my words accurate?* It is like trying to live up to a standard or put on a front to be a certain way; it could be a spiritual front or any image of how you want people to see you. That needs to be questioned as well.

Friend: I think that all my editing stuff kicks in. I think there are ways of saying things that are much more helpful than other ways. I am mentally editing myself as I speak, thinking that if I do that it will perhaps be more helpful.

David: There is a strain in observing words and behavior. The whole point of our discussion is to continually bring it back to the mind, to get in touch with the backwards and distorted fear-based thinking. It is not important what the behaviors or words are; we want to have a connection of minds where we can start looking at the ideas and beliefs. That is what we are doing. The subject/object split runs very deep. It covers so many things. We want to start to see that – to be aware, for example, of objectifying the recording equipment or the situation.

Friend: So when you say objectify, you just mean that I am making it apart from myself?

David: Yes. As soon as there is a subject and an object, then the mind has to make up a reason to be afraid. It has to protect the small me or the "self" that I see as apart from the world. It sees the world as encroaching upon it, weakening it. For instance, to use the example of the recording being shared – if there is a fear of people having judgments about it, that is a demonstration of the subject/object split. As soon as I believe there is something outside of me, then I have to immediately switch on a certain defensiveness to protect this small self that is apart from everything else.

## PROJECTION MAKES PERCEPTION

Friend: So how do I look at that? What attitude do I have to have in order to not objectify?

David: It is the intention, a willingness to step back in the mind and to begin to grasp that everything I perceive with my senses are simply thoughts in my own mind. *They are simply thoughts in my own mind.*

Friend: False thoughts?

David: Yes, unreal thoughts; thoughts that are not eternal and changeless. These are projections – ideas in my own mind that I have projected. Seeing that begins to give you the sense that there is an "I" that is distinct, whole, and capable of observing thoughts without believing in them.

Friend: So is it just the intention and willingness to look at it that way that is required?

David: Yes, the willingness to not order it. Let's freely associate with some ideas, for instance: *morning, chairs, microphone, woman, couch, sunshine*. Here we have a stream of thoughts that I verbalized. Now we want to get a sense of an observer or of something that is able to watch those thoughts without ordering them, without reading meaning into the thoughts.

For instance, *woman: sitting in chair, speaking into microphone, looking out at sunshine*. All of those thoughts have a reference point to the idea of "woman." The woman is the subject – the person with the eyes that are able to look at the microphone and the chairs and out at the sun. We have a subject/object split as opposed to those all, including the woman, being just a stream of thoughts in the mind, without any connection, without any association. In reality, it is impossible to link together or associate false thoughts but that is what the deceived mind attempts to do. It attempts to associate thought-forms and constructs with meaning based on those thought-forms. That is how the world's combinations of thought-forms were made up; projection makes perception.

## ASSOCIATION AND ORDERING OF THOUGHT-FORMS – GIVING MEANING WHERE THERE IS NONE

Friend: You went from naming "couch," "sunshine," and "microphone" to "woman sitting in the chair speaking in the microphone, looking out the window." Was the point just to say that there is an attempt to put individual components into some combination? That is what the mind tries to do – to take the isolated thought-forms, associate them and from that derive some kind of meaning or interpretation?

David: Yes, and it is false. The mind can attempt to do that but it just continues to sleep. It is trying to do something that cannot be done.

11

Friend: Because they are individual isolated thought-forms? Is that what you are saying?

David: They have no meaning in and of themselves.

Friend: Only in combination with other thought-forms do they seem to take on meaning.

David: When you think of a chair you immediately have all kinds of associations. You could say chairs are made for bodies to sit in, or there are different types of chairs or different weights of chairs. For example, when you go on a picnic you take a lawn chair as opposed to a reclining chair, which you would consider too heavy. The way that the ego – the deceived mind – works is that it has all kinds of meanings associated with everything in the world. Each thought-form is associated with all sorts of other thought-forms.

Friend: You are saying that we are moving toward a letting go of all of those associations?

David: Yes, letting go of *all* of those associations, because they are all very relative.

Friend: And variable, because your associations are different than my associations.

David: A child could grow up playing Little League Baseball and have a fondness for a particular wooden bat that he has played with for years. That same type of bat could have been used in a home in an abusive situation where a father went into tirades and knocked things down with it. He smashed the TV or hit some-body with it. The bat then has different associations for the child who lived in that home than for the other child who has fond memories of the smell of the wood or the crack of the bat as he hit a home run. The whole point is that they are *all* associations that are being made; they are all unreal.

Friend: That is why there is an attempt to let go of any association whatsoever? It is pretty inconceivable to my mind right now how it would be if I let go of all my associations with everything. I mean the very thought of it seems like it would be immensely chaotic, disorienting, disconcerting and unstable.

David: To the deceived mind, there is chaos perceived within – in other words, two thought systems that have no meeting point. There is a split that is very horrifying; that split gets projected out. The ordering of thought-forms is the mind's attempt to find order and sanity in the midst of the horror of it. But, by associating the thought-forms and reading meaning into them, the mind constructs its own version of reality based on these associations. This covers over the light in the mind which sees the sameness of everything. The ordering and associating of thought-forms obscures the sameness of the thought-forms. Regardless of what the thought-forms are, there is a meaning or a Purpose that can be given to them that is completely new and completely fresh every instant. It has nothing to do with the association of the thought-forms. It has nothing to do with the relative meanings that have been read into them.

There is an intensity when we come together – a purpose that can take over, replacing the self-consciousness that is censoring the words or is aware of the distraction of the microphone. Or, as in the example of the boys in the home where you are staying, there can be an intention, a purpose, that can take over that is fresh and new. The attention in the mind becomes focused; it becomes so single-minded such that whether the boys are running around or not, the noise just fades away. The mind is capable of focusing its attention on a different purpose. It is like speaking with someone in a crowd; you can focus your attention on the person you are speaking with and pull it away from all the background noise.

Friend: It seems the thing to do initially is to get very, very focused before beginning anything else, and to have the intention for that to be all that there is. I *have* experienced how powerful it is when everything else just fades away when I have a really strong intention and purpose. It fades away or comes to meet it, whichever way you want to look at it. That is all there is – that one intention – and everything is there to support it. Nothing can detract from it.

David: For there to be a conflict, there has to be opposition to something. You can see what freedom there is in this idea of transcending the subject/object split. If the mind can stay focused on that one intention and not become distracted or allow its attention to wander back to the *I'm a subject and this is the object* or, *This is the situation that I seem to be in* – if you can stay back in detachment from all those thought-forms, that purpose or intention can be held in mind.

All goals and expectations, everything that is strived for and all of the meanings that are read into the world spring from this subject/object split.

Friend: Is that just another way of speaking of the self-concept?

David: Yes.

## THE SELF-CONCEPT

Friend: So you could say that the self-concept becomes the point of reference for everything that is perceived.

David: Yes. The self-concept is a construction or a making up of these associated thought-forms; I perceive myself as a person. Where am I? I am a person in the living room, in a particular city, in a particular country on this particular planet, etc. The construct also includes reading meaning into "I am a body," such as male/female, educational backgrounds, social status, what language I speak, am I multilingual/bilingual; it goes on and on and on. There are stacks and stacks of meanings of the particular thought-forms that have been constructed in a specific way so as to make this small self appear to be unique and different from every other perceived form.

Friend: The particular configuration seems to define "my" self as different than and separate from "your" self.

David: That is where the conflict can arise. If I perceive "my" self as apart or different from "your" self, and "my" self is important in areas where our configurations of the world and our "selves" are different from one another, then we have differences of opinion. Then we have set up a situation where there is competition between us – something to fight about or something to prove or be right about. As soon as that is accepted as the intention, the sense of connectedness and oneness are immediately blocked from awareness.

From this point of view can you see how important it is to step back in the mind, away from those constructs, and let go of them? How is peace possible if everyone has a different construct of themselves and the differences are accentuated? There is a sense that if I give in to the way you see it all the time then there will not be any of me left. This of course leads to compromise: *I'll give in this much and you give in this much. We'll try to find a middle ground.* From the construct point of view there is a weakening of the self-concept because something is given up and compromised.

Friend: And usually only given up because it is perceived that what can be gained is greater than what is given up.

David: It is all in a perceptual sense too. One could say that in any type of marriage or collaboration there is a pooling of material resources, of skills, and of objects so that you have more than you had before. But we are right back to that idea of thought-form-associations. All thought-form associations are projections. Literally, the mind is whole and complete in a state where it does not project; it thinks only the thoughts that God created. It has no thoughts apart from God, which is pure abstraction. God is not associating thought-forms.

## PEACE IS LETTING GO OF THE SUBJECT/OBJECT SPLIT

David: This really gets to the core of any perceived problem in the world. If I am trying to attain or achieve something in the world, all my expectations arise from that configuration of thought-forms. All of the associations are an attempt to maintain the subject/object split – the idea that I am distinct and separate. Once you start to see the futility of that you can begin to dis-identify from the thought-forms and constructions. You can start to let go of those things without feeling that all will be chaos, for in fact all is peace when the subject/object split is let go of.

Friend: I noticed before when I was saying that it is impossible to let go of all those thought-form-associations, I was thinking of it in terms of all or nothing. You know, total wipe-out. It's never going to be that way; it is always going to be what the mind can let go of at any given time. In a way I don't have to fear that I have to, in a moment, let go of every single association. Ultimately I may, but my experience of it is that little by little I am able to let go.

David: The fear arises just from the intimation that in an instant it *could* all be let go of. When the mind becomes attached to the thought-form-associations and personhood – to this important person that it calls "me" – then it does seem like this is a leap into the void. *What will happen to me; who will I be if I am not who I think I am, if I am not this person in this world?* There is fear around that. The idea that I can do this piece by piece is a projection of the mind because of that fear. It is going to project the shift into time.

Friend: This is because it is believed as gentler as opposed to an abrupt, total sweep of things.

David: Yes, but that can be used as a metaphor for the mind: I can watch and gauge by my feelings. When I start to get off-center I can use that as a cue to pay attention, to train the mind. All the while there is an awareness that it just takes an instant, a vague awareness that it is all or nothing – that it can be let go of in *any* instant. To the split mind that is a fearful thing but as the mind starts to embrace that idea as a reality, then it is welcomed with joy.

One might think *Wow, it's a good thing I have got some time to think this thing out in a gradual way because it seems so enormous that I am just going to have to chip away at it piece by piece.* From another perspective, the Holy Spirit was given immediately as an answer to the separation. God is not giving you a torture chamber of time that you have to go through before you can finally accept that answer. The answer *has* been given.

Friend: So the idea that it can be gradual is just another construct of the mind?

David: Yes, which involves time, and time involves intervals which in reality do not exist.

## THE HOLY INSTANT – THE RELINQUISHMENT
## OF THE BELIEF IN PAST AND FUTURE

Friend: But is it a helpful construct?

David: Its helpfulness depends on the use to which it is put. We always have to look at the idea of purpose. If time is given over to the Holy Spirit's purpose then it is helpful. It is not seen as a trap or something that has to be escaped from, like *I can't wait to get this over with*. Time is used; it has been given to God's teachers – it is in their hands, it can be used by their minds. This gets into the idea of saving or collapsing time; it is given a connotation of being helpful. It is about this instant. *How do you feel right now?*

It is helpful to keep focusing on *how do I feel right now?* The Present is the aspect of time that touches on Eternity. But when time is used to maintain the separation – with the linear view of seeing past, present and future as continuous – then it is not helpful. In that view the past and future are given a sense of reality, of really existing. One can always find a reason to feel guilty by looking to the past and one can always find something to worry about when the future is believed in.

Friend: ...always looking for something to be different than the way it is.

David: The future, like the past, is a defense against the holy instant – the holy instant being that *all is perfect right now!* There is such a sense of rest, such a sense of stillness and contentment in that idea. When that idea is grasped and focused upon by the mind then all striving is let go of. The thought-form-associations we have been talking about are always past associations. They can be projected into a future but in that sense the past and future are both part of the thought-form associations. You need thought-form associations – a self-concept or a construct – before past and future can have any meaning; they are literally one and the same.

Friend: So with the undoing of the self-concept there is also the undoing of the whole linear time concept?

David: We can see that using your example. You said it seemed to make a difference whether this recording was something that just you would listen to as opposed to others listening to it. We are definitely talking about a future construct where not only is there a self apart from others (the subject/object split), but it has also been projected to the future, to how this recording will or will not be used. You said that there was some uneasiness along those lines. That thought is a projected thought, a self-concept thought. It is a thought of an association of what *may* happen. Two different constructs were made up; in the first it is just you, the small you, listening to the recording perhaps in the privacy of your own home. You can see that is a construct. The alternative could be that the recording is passed on to others to listen to, and that is another construct.

## Seeing the Construct as a Construct – the End of Ordering

David: We are talking about ordering of thoughts. As an example we have here two different constructs where one seems more favorable than the other. The construct is not recognized as a construct when there is an ordering. The escape from all concepts and constructs is to literally sink beneath them in the mind – to literally not order and configure the thought-forms but to merely recognize them and step back to see the bigger picture. The biggest picture you could possibly imagine would be a construct of the cosmos seen as an entire fabric without any ordering.

Friend: So it ceases to be a construct? It is only the ordering – seeing the fragmented parts as separate from each other – that really makes it the construct that it is. Once that is removed from it then it really is no longer a construct?

David: I think it would be more accurate to say that it is then *seen* as a construct. But as long as there is ordering going on, it seems real. It seems like I really am a person in a world. I have a family and a job. I have possessions. I have, say, two cars; one is a 1968 Plymouth and one is a 1992 Camaro. Perhaps I value one more than the other. It is the valuing – the ordering of the thoughts-forms in the construct – that obscures the fact that it is just a construct. Ordering also obviously maintains the subject/object split. There is a separating involved. There is the thought that I am a person, and then there is this vast world/universe/cosmos. Here you have the old *individual versus society*, or the *individual versus the universe* kind of split going on. There is great importance placed on this personhood.

Friend: My mind keeps grasping for ways of understanding the subject/object split because I notice that even just the use of these words seems very abstract to me. It helps me to think of it in terms of self-concept. What are some other ways of framing or talking about this – using different words?

David: It runs very deep. For example, the scientific method of identifying a problem, gathering data and performing an experiment; it implies the subject/object, the observer and the observed. Part of the scientific method is the observation. Observation with the body, whether you are using a microscope, a telescope or the naked eye, involves a subject, which is the observer, and an object, which is the observed.

## THE OBSERVER AND THE PERSONHOOD

Friend: So how does that relate to mind-watching and *wanting* to be in the observer role?

David: The Observer, with a capital "O," is the Mind. This Mind is able to observe the thoughts, as opposed to the subject/object or the observer/observed when we are talking about personhood. The observer in observer/observed is the "small o" observer. It is a person, a peeping Tom, like a scientist who is observing certain phenomena or a housewife who is observing and watching her children. It involves the belief that I am a person. Whenever there is a belief in personhood, we are still with the small *o*.

But the mind can be trained to watch *all* thoughts go by – the whole stream of thoughts – without the assumption of personhood. The mind can be trained to step back to see the big picture, to see that the belief in personality traits such as *I'm shy, I'm aggressive, I'm beautiful or handsome by worldly standards, I'm good at math, I'm not so good at baseball*, etc., are all thoughts in the mind. It can step back and just watch the entire stream of consciousness.

Friend: And that implies an identification with the "capital S" Self, whereas the other one would be the "small s" self.

David: At the beginning this can seem very difficult; the mind can have thoughts that there is no "capital O" Observer back there. The mind might think, *There are just all these thoughts; my mind is crazy* or it might think, *I can't observe.* That is where the practice comes in. Dis-identifying takes practice because the mind believes that it *is* those thoughts.

Friend: So how do you practice it? I mean, how would you even describe to somebody how you practice this?

## Mind Training

David: Initially it is usually just something as simple as sitting down and closing the body's eyes and attempting to take hold of particular ideas from the Course, like the lesson for the day – as a point of attention. The mind is untrained at this point. It wanders and jumps around; it is frantic. If someone honestly starts to look at their mind in an untrained state, they see a very chaotic, frantic state. In the early stages it is good to have a particular idea for the day, such as one from the Course. In other traditions they are called mantras or affirmations.

Friend: Something to refocus the mind with when it notices that it has wandered.

David: These are the early stages. Practicing like this can go on for quite some time but with persistence there is a sense of a calming down, a sense of a settling into Stillness. Not to say that the chaotic stage will not seem to come back, but at first the words and the mantras are very helpful. As one proceeds along, there is more and more of a sense that this is not a separate activity requiring for example that the eyes be closed or that the body be in a particular place or a specific posture.

Friend: So it is no longer about taking time out and sitting down for a particular exercise? It is more ongoing.

David: The mind is becoming more aware that the inner world of thoughts and the outer world of projected images are not different. As the mind starts to get this then the idea of meditating by finding a place to be undisturbed and closing the eyes starts to fade because you know that is a thought-form as well. It is more like a carpet ride or a flow of being, flowing down a river, just bobbing along and being carried by a flow in the mind whereby you can watch. You do not feel an attachment to things, to outcomes, to the form turning out in a particular way.

Peace of mind as a goal is an abstract goal. It is not a quantifiable goal. You cannot measure peace of mind and you cannot describe it. The mind will still attempt to do and say things like *I am more peaceful when I am walking in a park than when I am driving in the city* or, *I am more peaceful when I am in meditation than when I am at my parent's house*. It still wants to make categories. Ultimately there has to be a complete dis-identification from the way the script of the world is going.

This does not mean retreating from the world in the sense of trying to run and hide. For some this sounds boring or difficult to even comprehend how one could live without ordering thoughts, making judgments and striving after things. But really, in the ultimate sense, it is about stepping back from the thought-forms in the mind. There is no dependence on what the body is doing or is not doing, because the body is a thought-form. We are talking at another level now.

Friend: It has nothing to do with form.

David: Right.

Friend: We are talking at a level strictly of the mind; the form will follow as it will always follow the content of the mind.

David: The form is *seen* as a construct. When the thought-forms are ordered they seem real; *I am a real person in a real world, with real problems.* But when you are mind-watching with the "capital O" observer, watching with the "capital Y" You – the witness-Self, the "capital S" Self – the entire world and cosmos are seen as constructs.

Friend: And it is only by seeing a construct as real that I would even have questions such as *What do I do? What about a job? What about whatever?* Those questions rest on a belief that the construct is real.

## WHO ASKS THE QUESTION AND WHAT IS THE PROBLEM?

David: The construct is asking the question.

Friend: Yes, I am seeing that.

David: It is the small self that is concerned about a job, or family issues, or capital punishment, or even about the one saying *I am this little person and I'm all screwed up and I don't have it together like so and so!* In order to make comparisons you have to have a subject/object split. There is ordering involved with comparison; the construct is asking the questions. And those questions are not really questions, they are statements. When you say *I have a problem with my boss* or *I have a problem with my daughter*, it is really the construct asking the question. *What's wrong with my relationship? What's wrong with my life?* It is the construct asking the question, or you could say that the construct is making the statement that it is a construct! This is because the construct is not seen as a construct. This brings us around full circle to defining the problem. Even if the problem has been solved, how can one know that it has been solved if one has not been able to see what the problem is?

Friend: It seems like once we can really see what the problem is, what seemed to be the problem does not seem like a problem. There is no problem.

David: That is a fact: There is no problem.

Friend: Because every perceived problem is the belief in separation and there is no separation. Is that what you are saying?

David: Yes.

Friend: So there is no problem; there are only *seeming* problems.

David: Once the construct is seen as a construct, the split is healed because there is no subject/object split any more. The problem has been seen as a problem in the mind. The split was in the mind; once it has been given up—once it has been seen that it is not a fact—then there is no problem. The key idea we started with is that you first have to see the problem as being in the mind. Once it is recognized that the split is in the mind—not out in the world—then there is no problem.

Friend: So why doesn't it seem that easy to do? I guess because the mind does not want to see that the problem is not out in the world; it does not want to see that it is right here in the mind?

# Who Am I?

David: If it doesn't seem easy, there has to be an investment in that construct and those thought-form associations. Why is there such a strong investment in it? There is investment because there is fear. There is fear that if I give up ordering my thoughts, if I give up the construct of who I think I am as a person and all my meanings, associations and conclusions, there will be loss involved and that would be scary. Somehow the construct is serving me. It has value to me and so why would I want to step back in the mind to see the bigger picture? Why would I want to question the construct if I still believe that it serves me?

Friend: There wouldn't be any motivation. There is no point in fixing what is not broken.

David: It could all just seem too abstract, so let's approach it from the level of feelings. Do you feel complete, stable peace in your life or is it a rollercoaster ride? Do you have fluctuating emotions where you sometimes feel peaceful or joyful and other times upset, irritated, guilty, jealous, and fearful? Can you take an honest look at your life and recognize that you do not feel a constant, consistent, stable state of peace? If you do not, perhaps there is something here that needs to be looked at. Or do you prefer to just minimize the demons, manage the neurosis and persist in a general state of unhappiness?

Friend: Instead of particular miserableness.

David: We are coming to a point where we can start to realistically see the hope of completely bringing an end to all sense of upset, disorder, and chaos. It is a phenomenal proposition! To do so requires the questioning of the constructs. It requires that the mind let go of those thought-form associations.

Friend: And you cannot let go of them unless you see that they are there.

David: Right. And you cannot see that they are there if you believe that you *are* them – that you are the construct.

Friend: So the dialogue helps to uncover, disclose, and expose the constructs?

David: It helps the mind see *Oh, I thought that was me, but I am not that*. It helps to step back and to dis-identify from that which it thought it was. And there is immense joy with that. Strain and stress is lifted from the mind. By holding onto the construct and the thought-form associations, the mind was denying its natural abstract state, its state of freedom. By being able to step back and dis-identify from the false construct, the mind is released to its natural state; it feels a stable sense of peace and joy.

Friend: It takes a lot of energy to hold in place an idea of my "self" that is not my Self. I can see how freeing it is to just let go of all the garbage that I have tacked on.

## Letting Go the Ways of the World

David: In the early stages it is frightening because there seems to be a letting go of the ways of the world. The world teaches "bigger," "better," "faster," "more." Upward mobility, for instance, is a commonly held belief or goal, as is competition.

Friend: It feels kind of scary to think about stepping out of viable ways of the world that have become so familiar.

David: It comes back to a sense of security. The mind has placed its identity in the constructs; from their perspective it seems ludicrous to step out of ambition. The construct says you will die. From within the belief system of the self-concept, of scarcity, giving up striving and fighting and everything that goes along with that, means that you will be swallowed up by the so-called external world – which is itself a construct.

Friend: Yes, we have been taught that it is only by setting goals, working hard and going for it that you can get your fair share and stay ahead of the game, that you can keep your head above water. What you are saying is that when you let go of that construct or self-concept you are also letting go of all those kinds of goals. You are actually replacing those goals with the one goal, which is being at peace.

David: A unified goal of peace. We are not saying that the laying aside of the self-concept is a process without a goal. It has a goal, an abstract one: peace of mind! There is no thought-form associated with that goal. That can be seen as very ambiguous and abstract to a mind that is conditioned to pursue concrete goals that are desirable in the world's eyes. But that is in effect what this is about; worldly goals are laid aside for the one goal of peace.

Friend: Do you want to say anything about your experience of doing that?

David: Well, there was plenty of doubting along the way but it has been an experience of feeling impelled to step back and step back and step back in my mind.

## SEEING THE PATHS THAT LEAD NOWHERE

Friend: What impelled you?

David: It was not anything external; it has been a calling from deep within, reminding me that there is something more than all of this. There was a sense of disillusionment after having sought out so many external things that I thought would bring meaning to my life, but didn't. One metaphor for it is to imagine a lot of wheels, like in those old watches. They are of all different sizes and there are wheels inside of wheels, inside of wheels. There is a stepping back from all of it, hopping out of it and noticing you were *on* a wheel, pursuing something that was very circular that did not get you where you thought it would; you just kept going round and round. I stepped back and saw the wheels, saw that I was just going round and round on one wheel or another, and that there was no fulfillment in any of it. I went deep into looking at what was seemingly being pursued, whether it was possessions, or a specific kind of relationship, career or climate, or associations with specific kinds of people, feeling more valuable or more alive with *these* people than with *those* people….

Friend: …specific kind of activities, pastimes, entertainment, enjoyment….

David: Right. The body evolved in many different ways – skills and abilities were developed; there was always a desire to improve and improve. One wheel gets outgrown, and then another and another. I experienced this call, a pull to go back, back, back in the mind and to start to really question my values. I searched for meaning in life, in religion, science, politics, even entertainment – each was pursued with the hope that this will *do* it. Repeatedly I saw *that's not it*, and that is not it, and that is not it either!

Stepping back further and further in the mind leads one beyond the physical, into the metaphysics – into an investigation of how the mind works and what perceptions, emotions, thoughts, beliefs and assumptions really are. And even that is something that has to be stepped back from – that sense of studying the mind as if you can objectify the mind as something *other than.* Ultimately there comes this pull, this awareness, to leap from that subject/object split. Even if I am able to talk about the mind and describe it but I still see it as something objective, then there is still that split.

There is a state of being which is just recognition of what *is;* in a metaphorical sense you know it is not "I" that lives, it is the Christ that lives in me. The sense of duality disappears. There is no sense of objectifying behavior, of wondering what you should or should not do. The analyzing stops. Spirit is placed at the center. Spirit is valued. Attention is placed on the Spirit or the Voice for God or the intuition – however you want to talk about it. There is clear focus and intention; everything else follows from that. There is no attention put on the construct anymore but all attention is simply directed to staying in the witness-mode or the Observer mode if you will.

Friend: So in that state there is no need to struggle over decisions, it just all unfolds effortlessly?

David: "A decision is a conclusion based on everything that you believe." (T-24.in.2) You step back and begin to see that the beliefs are part of the construct; then you step back deeper and deeper and deeper to a point that is beyond the beliefs. There is an abstract state of being that is literally beyond belief, beyond thought-form associations and beyond constructs. There is rest in that state. There is contentment. There are no alternatives in that state of being. There is nothing to choose between.

Friend: That is the Atonement, right?

David: It just *is*. Yes.

Friend: Then you can see that there are no alternatives.

## PEACE – SEEING THE CONSTRUCT
## AS A CONSTRUCT

David: That is seeing the construct as a construct. That is seeing that there is nothing outside of me – really understanding that ideas leave not their source. The world was an idea in my mind and it did not leave its source. The subject/object disappears. There is such an awareness of connectedness that all those constructs and differences are gone, of body and hand and leaf and tree and butterfly; there is just One. It is all just One. The time/space universe is seen as a single fabric; there are no particular threads that are separated out as more or less valuable. Categorizing, organizing, analyzing, and dissecting – all that is stopped; all that was a defense against this state of being, against the fact of what is.

Friend: You are saying that seeing all the little pieces is the mind's defense against seeing the totality? Kind of like with a jigsaw puzzle, as long as you keep focusing on individual pieces you cannot see the whole picture?

David: Yes, the pieces imply subject and object. By talking about *parts* we are back in duality and multiplicity. Seeing the whole fabric is not like seeing it through the body's eyes of course, because there is the duality again.

Friend: The body's eyes *can't* see the whole thing. Is that what you are saying?

David: Right. When I say "see the fabric," that is just a metaphor for *All is One*. There is no split between subject and object or observer and observed. There is nothing to defend in that state because there is nothing to defend against! You need duality to have something to oppose. Seeing the construct or the fabric is a state of being; it is not a worldly sense of seeing. In the worldly sense of seeing you can climb up to the 15th floor of a skyscraper and see so much more than you could down on the street. You can go up to the 30th floor and see even more. You can go to the very top and see the horizon – a much different perspective – but this is *not* the seeing of the whole fabric because it is still perceptual. It is a broader perspective, more expansive perhaps, but it is still perceptual.

You can go up in an airplane and see an even more expansive perspective; you could go up in a space shuttle and see the globe! You could get pictures back from a satellite that was sent from Mars and see yet an even more expansive perspective. But these views are all perceptual; all of these perspectives imply personhood. They can all be seen through the body's eyes; they all involve constructs. They are just shifts within the construct. But there comes a point when the mind is aware that the entire cosmos is a construct. Duality ends; I am no longer a little person in a city, in a country, in a world, in a solar system, in a cosmos.

Perception always requires a perceiver and something that is perceived. There is a state in which this is no longer the case; perception is literally laid aside. It no longer serves. It no longer has value. You may say that you like the world and what your eyes perceive. It really comes down to honestly looking at your life with all its fluctuating emotions – the loneliness and isolation or just the insatiable restlessness – and asking yourself what you really want. Do you want peace of mind?

Friend: I guess the question is, above all else, what do I want? And if I think that above all else what I want is what I see in this world with these eyes, then I probably will keep going with that until I get tired of trying to find something there that isn't, and come around to wanting peace now, above all else. How do I go about that?

David: There is openness in the mind. There is an opening in the mind that seems to be so determined to make something of itself, to make something *more* of itself – the mind that is so determined to hang on to "individuality," "uniqueness," and "separation." There is a thought that there has to be something beyond all of this.

Friend: For me that opening came when I felt like I was really in a pit in my life. Just out of sheer desperation there was a willingness to open up to something else.

## LET ME RECOGNIZE THE PROBLEM HAS BEEN SOLVED

David: Let's read Workbook lesson 80:

> If you are willing to recognize your problems, you will recognize that you have no problems. Your one central problem has been answered and you have no other. Therefore, you must be at peace. Salvation thus depends on recognizing this one problem and understanding that it has been solved. One problem, one solution. Salvation is accomplished. Freedom from conflict has been given you. Accept that fact, and you are ready to take your rightful place in God's plan for salvation.

Your only problem has been solved. Repeat this over and over to yourself today with gratitude and conviction. You have recognized your own problem, opening the way for the Holy Spirit to give you God's answer. You have laid deception aside and seen the light of truth. You have accepted salvation for yourself by bringing the problem to the answer. And you can recognize the answer, because the problem has been identified.

You are entitled to peace today. A problem that has been resolved cannot trouble you. Only be certain you do not forget that all problems are the same. Their many forms will not deceive you while you remember this. One problem, one solution. Accept the peace this simple statement brings.

In our longer practice periods today, we will claim the peace that must be ours when the problem and the answer have been brought together. The problem must be gone, because God's answer cannot fail. Having recognized one, you have recognized the other. The solution is inherent in the problem. You are answered and have accepted the answer. You are saved.

Now let the peace that your acceptance brings be given you. Close your eyes, and receive your reward. Recognize that your problems have been solved. Recognize that you are out of conflict, free and at peace. Above all, remember that you have one problem, and that the problem has one solution. It is in this that the simplicity of salvation lies. It is because of this that it is guaranteed to work.

Assure yourself often today that your problems have been solved. Repeat the idea with deep conviction, as frequently as possible. And, be particularly sure to apply the idea for today to any specific problem that may arise. Say quickly:

Let me recognize this problem has been solved.

Let us be determined not to collect grievances today. Let us be determined to be free of problems that do not exist. The means is simple honesty. Do not deceive yourself about what the problem is, and you must recognize it has been solved. (W-80)

David: "Let me recognize my problems have been solved." This gets at what we were talking about; the construct – the self-concept – is past tense. To see it as it really is, is to see it as past, as over, as done! If you are willing to recognize your problem you will recognize that you *have* no problem! Your one central problem has been answered and you have no other. Therefore you must be at peace.

## IDENTITY CONFUSION

David: If I do not feel at peace then it is a case of mistaken identity. I have identified with the construct. That is the problem, and I can change my mind.

Friend: That is always the problem, isn't it? It is always identity confusion.

David: It is always identity confusion and it is always remedied with a decision, with a remembrance, *Oops, that's the problem and I can change my mind.* The Atonement is a permanent change of mind. You can choose to forgive, you can choose a miracle. It seems like there are times when the mind does not choose the miracle and seems to be in a state of unrest or upset; that is part of the construct in and of itself. It is a fluctuating self that can at times remember its wholeness and at other times cannot. The Atonement is the fact of *all or nothing*. It is a permanent awareness. The fluctuation ends. "This course will be believed entirely or not at all." (T-22.II.7) Suddenly you can understand the meaning of statements like that.

> ...Salvation thus depends on recognizing there is *one* problem, and understanding that it has been solved. One problem, one solution. Salvation is accomplished. Freedom from conflict has been given you. Accept that fact, and you are ready to take your rightful place in God's plan for salvation.
>
> Your only problem has been solved! Repeat this over and over to yourself today with gratitude and conviction. You have recognized your only problem, opening the way for the Holy Spirit to give you God's answer. You have laid deception aside, and seen the light of truth. You have accepted salvation for yourself by bringing the problem to the answer and you can recognize the answer because the problem has been identified. (W-80.1-2)

What a phenomenal release!

Friend: Yes, that is the word that came to my mind too. What a release!

David: Is this practical? Is peace of mind practical? That is the question that the mind must answer. This is an eminently practical course. It is aimed at revealing the simplicity of salvation, the simplicity of peace of mind. It is a tool for helping the mind cut through its own deception, its own beliefs about itself that circumscribe and limit it, keeping it bound in awareness – not in reality, but in this awareness. This is the good news. This is the gospel that Jesus came to teach to set man free.

Friend: This is the Hurrah! Hallelujah! Identity crisis is not something that occurs when you turn forty. It is something that occurs and is perpetuated in the mind until Atonement is accepted – until the mind wakes up to Who and What it is.

David: That is a description of it and a metaphor for describing the process. The attention needs to be focused on the mind and my decision, this moment! The attention is splintered when the mind is riveted on past and future thoughts, in other words on the construct/concept. It sees itself as within that construct. There is no escape for it; there is no relief for a mind that is identified with a concept like that. If you take this line of thinking and run it out in any realm of life, you can start to see the implications of perceived problems whether it is in relationships, finances, economics, scarcity, etc.

Friend: Would you like to run it out for one of those?

David: Do you have a particular avenue?

Friend: Well, I think everyone at some point has that show up in relationship. Why don't we run it out in relationship?

## FALSE RELATIONSHIPS –
## THE SUBSTITUTES FOR LOVE

David: OK. Let's start with the metaphysics. Let's give the whole topic of relationships a basis or a metaphysical underpinning; there is one problem and it is misidentification. In Biblical terms we could call it "the fall of man" or "the fall from Grace." To forsake one's identity as God created oneself in Spirit is *the fall.*

Believing that such a thing is possible – investing in this puff of madness – is where the split or the Big Bang seemed to occur. When we speak of relationship in this world we think of it as involving persons and bodies.

Friend: Here we go, subject/object again.

David: We are back to subject/object, whether we define the relationship as mother/daughter, mother/son or father/daughter, father/son or as a relationship between lovers, friends, acquaintances, neighbors, peers, siblings, etc. These are different constructs. *Love is One.* There are not different kinds of love. There is just one experience of love. To fragment it and think that there are different kinds of love is to make up a construct of something as a substitute for the true experience of Oneness. The projected world was made as a defense *against* love. As soon as the split seemed to occur, as soon as the tiny mad idea – the ego, the lie – was taken seriously instead of laughed at, then a defense was needed. The mind believed that it was guilty, that it had usurped the power of God. The ego projected out a world to hide in and told the mind that the world could now be its home.

Friend: And God won't come into form. He will never find you here.

David: God is Spirit, eternal and changeless. Form is finite, fragmented, limited, specific, and particular. He cannot come in here; you can hide. This is where the misidentification and the investment in relationships enter in, as they are perceived in this world. There is the subject/object split. If I am in a deceived state, I believe I am a person. And along with the belief in personhood there is always a deep sense of loneliness, upset, loss, guilt and fear in the mind from making up something that was false and denying wholeness–denying the true Self as Christ. That is why there is such a searching and craving for love, for Mr. Right, for someone to trust.

Friend: To reverse these feelings of isolation.

David: Yes, to solve my loneliness problem. It is not seen that the problem is the belief in personhood; the problem is that a construct has been made up of being a person in a world, alone and empty, seeking to find fulfillment outside oneself, just like all the other persons are doing.

Friend: The training has been that this is just the way it is; it's natural, or normal. People come together around common interests, common values, common purposes, common goals....

David: It is quite sneaky in the sense that if I have a construct that I am a person and I like America and I like the city, I like fine dining and sports and cuddling up and watching movies–if I find another person, so called, who likes the same things, then wow! It seems like a match made in Heaven. Though I have made up a construct of a world and a self that is little, the littleness doesn't seem so bad now because I have found another self that agrees with me on this.

Friend: Complementary littleness.

David: And it reinforces my construct as being true. It is sneaky, very sneaky. In a sense it is a match made in Heaven; it is Heaven on earth for the ego because now the form has been raised as a substitute for the abstract Spirit and the deception has been bought into–it doesn't seem so horrifying and traumatic. I have run away from Spirit and seem now to have made up a state where I can find happiness by getting something outside myself.

Friend: There's a substitution taking place. The mind is substituting that for Heaven, for God.

David: It takes all its happiness eggs and puts them into this basket of "other," this love partner, special friend, etc. It can even be objectified into a car, or a boat, a house or even rifles; you know, take your pick.

Friend: A sports team that I root for....

David: Yes, it does not matter what the concept is. These are thought-form associations; the mind is very identified with this substitute because....

Friend: ...it *seems* to give it everything it wants.

David: And now I do not have to remember about that light back in the mind that keeps calling and reminding me of my abstract reality. I can dissociate from that, completely forget that light and get very caught up in the form-relationship. Another aspect of it is that I need my special people because the flipside of personhood is that there are going to be those persons that are not supportive of this construct that I have made. They seem to see the whole construct in a different way. If part of my construct is "pro-life" and I feel very strongly about that and another person seems to be vehemently "pro-choice," then there is a conflict there. This is not a friend; this is someone who is seen as attempting to weaken my values. *One of us has to be right*, the ego says. *I need to convince that other person that they are wrong, because I am right.* You could apply that to any issue that you can think of. It gets played out in relationships in that I find my special friends – the people that will agree with me. I surround myself with those who share the same values and I distance or segregate myself from people with different values.

Friend: There is this whole idea of belonging, of wanting to feel that I belong; it could be a family, a team, a church or even a country. The deceived mind desperately wants to be associated with something that supports and reinforces the construct of itself that it has made up.

David: It is very important because the only other resource would be to turn within and start to question everything one values, to start to dig deep into the mind. Of course the ego will say not to dare do that; *you'll be obliterated, you'll be destroyed if you go back to the beginning.* The ego's assumption of the separation is that it is real – that it has occurred. The ego counsels that you have usurped God's power and if you go back towards that light you will pay for what you have done. It is all imaginary. Beneath the ego and the belief in separation is the awareness of the Joy that is possible. You cannot separate from your Father. You can choose not to be aware of truth but you cannot change truth. Truth *is.*

## MONEY AND LACK – PROBLEMS FOR THE CONSTRUCT

David: OK, that was about relationships, now let's look at finances. Money is an interchangeable medium of value in the world. Every split or fragment in mind seems to have a different construct of the world. According to the ego's counsel, there has to be some segment or unit of measurement for exchange. Money is a symbol of that; that is why it is so highly valued.

We are back to the subject/object split; if I believe I am a person then I believe I have rights. I believe that I am a body that can go places, achieve something and accumulate things. All this is part of the construct. Money is seen as very valuable as far as the construct is concerned. It is very high on the hierarchy of forms because it is so interchangeable. It is believed that it can bring me what I want, what I – the person – wants.

Friend: That's where the identity confusion comes in again.

David: Yes. Persons are associated with specific forms such as status, possessions, position, even climates, and money is very much associated with their worth; there is much concern about money because it seems to impinge on a person's value. It is a question of identity; the identity is tied up in the money because it is an interchangeable symbol that represents many things. Lots of things can seemingly be attained with money, so there is enormous strain that the mind goes through regarding finances. It is still the same conceptual problem – the construct of subject and object; when that dissolves there is obviously no need for money because there is no more need of the world.

Friend: It is the construct-self that has a need for money or anything money can buy? Is that what you are saying?

David: The construct is a construct of lack. To deny your Selfhood as the Christ and to accept instead a false self that has been made up is to accept the belief in lack. If I believe I am a person then I am lacking. Just take a look at all the simple forms of lack: I am lacking warmth, I need to put a coat on. I am lacking coolness so I need to take some clothes off. There is lack of food or water; I need something to quench my thirst. I am lacking love; I need people to stroke me and touch me and love me.

Friend: Affirm me; validate me.

David: *Encourage me, support me. I am lacking prestige or position or respect. I want and need that. I need awards and recognition.*

Friend: You are saying that every one of those things is not real; it is all part of the construct?

David: It is all part of the construct. Money is tied in with the world, with prestige, with status, with freedom of the body. With money the small "I," the body, the personal "me," can move around in this fictional world; it can go where it wants to go and do what it wants to do. There is a whole menu of ways that the construct has contrived to have the "good life," a menu of the pleasures of the world. And it is all a big deception because the guilt of believing in such a construct is concealed in the mind. The mind *seems* to be having an experience of things working out well in this world of form, even though it is really hallucinating.

Friend: So the guilt is hidden and held in place. It is perpetuated in the mind?

David: It does not go away. Even when the person seems to be getting all the good things in life, all the fine dining, comforts, and respect, there are still those doggone things like sickness and moody periods of loneliness that break into this nice illusionary dream-world of happiness and satisfaction. Or sometimes it is the other way around. There may be addictions or extreme scarcity involving a constant struggle to survive. Instead of the scarcity being "handled" with illusions of security it is experienced as being very real. The world is constructed in such a way that the world witnesses to the belief in lack and unworthiness. It is the same in that it still comes from the mind's belief in the construct; it is the other end of the same spectrum.

Friend: So the world is always either witnessing to the lack or covering over the belief in lack?

David: Correct. The construct is filling up the hole with something in the world, or wishing to fill it, wishing to solve the problem with external means, like with a lottery ticket. So-called low income people just line up hoping for that big score. The belief is still there, the belief that something outside myself can fill me up.

Friend: So that is how they are really the same; behind both manifestations is the belief that wealth and power will make a difference. They will fill up the void of emptiness that I feel.

David: Yes, though that generalization does not cover everyone. There are those who disdain wealth and possessions. You could call them ascetics. There is still a belief in personhood but in this case the belief is that if the body is denied, somehow that will mitigate the punishment that is deserved. The subject/object split is held onto but now instead of it being valuable and favorable to collect possessions there is dissociation. It is more valuable to be poor. Again, it is just a different construct. It is not the escape from the construct which sees that it is all made up. Personhood has to be questioned; it has to be stepped back from.

Friend: So is there any construct that is any more viable or helpful than any other construct?

David: There is one construct that is more valuable; that is forgiveness. Forgiveness is the construct of stepping back, back, back to the point where you can see it all as a construct. You have stepped back so far that you only have the purpose of healing and wholeness in the mind. All of the judgment and valuing, all of the ordering of the thought-forms is gone; there is no hierarchy among them. There is no meaning read into them and no associations made.

There is a blanket that covers all the thought-forms in one metaphor; the cosmos is seen as a single fabric with no particular threads singled out as more or less valuable. Forgiveness is a meaning in the mind that is given to everything in form. It still is a construct in the sense that it is perceptual; it is the one helpful construct – the one all-inclusive construct where there is no ordering among the thought-forms.

Friend: What about other constructs? Doesn't the Course say something about changing concepts as you go along, saying that as you let go of one concept you will move to a more expansive one, until you finally get to the point where you let go of all of them? In that sense, isn't the construct that is broader more helpful than the one that you left?

## FORGIVENESS – THE VOLUNTARY RELINQUISHMENT OF ALL CONSTRUCTS

David: The only value that can be put on a construct or form of any kind is, "What is it for?"

There can be helpful stepping stones along the way. Reincarnation for example; there is an idea that a soul is immortal but keeps returning again and again to the world, learning lessons until it finally has remembered itself and seen past the veil of illusion. The concept of reincarnation can be helpful if it gives one a sense of the eternal, of something that is beyond the temporal world – but it is still a construct in the sense that it involves the belief in the birth and death of bodies. We call them "lifetimes"; there is a linear sense to it. It is obviously still part of the construct of the world because it involves all the temporal things of time, space, birth, death, and bodies – yet it can be a helpful stepping-stone.

Friend: Doesn't the mind keep expanding even within what is called a single lifetime? I guess that depends on our purpose of undoing and unlearning and examining things so that you can see the construct and step back from it. It seems that the construct in the mind keeps changing, keeps loosening up, keeps letting go of more and more of what it once thought it was.

David: It is like the wheels we were talking about, where you outgrow one and step back. Though the mind seems to still be on a wheel, it can see the smaller wheels within it. Forgiveness in that sense would be the largest wheel, outside of all the other wheels. It looks in on them all, asking the question, "What is helpful?" This is the way the undoing process works. The Holy Spirit and the higher mind work with the beliefs in the lower mind; it is for the lower mind to voluntarily give up these beliefs. The mind increasingly starts to see that there are no accidents. Every situation can be seen differently by asking what is most helpful or, "What is it for?" The purpose or the intent is to lay aside all concepts, all images, and all thoughts of self, of God and of the world that are part of the construct.

Friend: And that is only in Atonement, isn't it?

David: Yes.

## THE WILLINGNESS TO LEARN OF REAL RELATIONSHIP

Friend: I want to go back to the relationship issue again and pick up from where we left it. Having exposed relationships as a substitute for God or for going within – where do I go from here? What do I do with this information? I *am* going to be in relationship; in a way it's like I cannot *not* be in relationship. Another thing is that I do not really know what relationship is. I do not remember my experience of true relationship, which is relationship with the Father. That is really what relationship is, not what I have defined as relationship in terms of this world.

David: There is a discovery to be made here. You just made two opposing statements. The first was, "I cannot *not* be in relationship," and the second: "I don't know what relationship is." There is an incongruity there. It has to be one or the other; either you understand relationship or you do not. The second statement opens the mind to a willingness to learn, to allow the Holy Spirit to teach you the meaning of true relationships.

Instead of projecting that you know what relationship is, the opportunity is to come together in a joining of mind with the intent of not knowing: *I want to learn; I want to see differently.* It really is no different than anything we have discussed so far since it is about the subject/object split. When there is a subject/object split – when the mind has split itself off into those two parts – then there is no relationship because the mind has denied its identity. Only in its true identity is the mind in real relationship.

Friend: So relationship is mistakenly associated with two-ness? Real relationship can only be associated with oneness? I talk about being in relationship with *someone else*. There is the two-ness already. Obviously I do not know what relationship is if I am thinking about it in terms of myself relating to someone else.

David: The mind is one. When we speak of the mind as one, we can still speak of causation – of cause and effect. There is not two-ness in cause and effect because they are inseparable.

Friend: And simultaneous, right?

David: Right. To be an effect there has to be a cause; to be a cause one has to have an effect. They are interdependent. We are getting into the realm of the mind and Creation. The Father and the Son are of one will and of one mind. The Father is the *Cause* and the Son is the *Effect*. The Father is the *Prime Creator* and the Son is the *Creation*. The Son, being like the Father, is a co-Creator;

he is capable of creating, of *extending* his will as the Father does. We are speaking in that sense of One Mind. There is no distinctive difference between the Father and the Son other than in the function of Creation. The Father created the Son and the Son did not create the Father. Once we get into the realm of the error of separation, projected out in the world, then we have specifics. Then there is the sense of duality and two-ness where we have *specific* differences. That is what relationship in this world is thought to be. Once again, it is a construct. It is a relationship between my *person* and my house, my person and my wife's person or my child's person, my person and objects—my car, my school, my sports team, my clothes, my skills, my intelligence, etc. There is a sense of a separate, individual self; *all* relationships in this world are special in that sense. It is not really relationship at all. They are all thought-form-associations. It is a relationship or a relative construct of meaning that has no meaning at all.

## HOLY RELATIONSHIP

Friend: So what about holy relationship?

David: Holy relationship is to step back and not judge the constructs, to withdraw the mind from them. It is still a metaphor. Think of it as two minds with the single intent of consistently holding in mind that the entire world is a construct, to not let anything come between them, so to speak. There is no personal interest in the sense of separate selves but there is still use of the word "relationship" as if there are persons. Each person looks within and sees the wholeness and completeness within themselves and therefore does not feel lacking. There is no sense of needing to get something or wanting to bargain with the other person. Obviously this is still a concept and a construct because we are still talking about personhood and persons but it is a very high construct because it is not based on lack. It is a construct that is pointing towards the resolution of subject and object.

Friend: That would be one of those more helpful constructs.

David: Yes, a phenomenal learning accomplishment, as the Course says. It takes a lot of mind training to give up one's investment in a personal small self. Metaphorically, two people who have that as their focus or intention are moving towards a holy relationship where they give up all the bargaining and reciprocity, all the seeking of someone to please them, to gratify them, or to satisfy them in some way.

Friend: So the focus is solely on that one intent, and that is what makes it possible to not have any personal interest enter in.

David: The one intent is to step back and be the observer – to not have personal interest. When differences do seem to come up or when the mind is upset it is seen as an opportunity to openly talk about it. There is a willingness to lay things out on the table and tell it as it is perceived and to support each other. When something is up for healing it is about seeing that it is just another belief that is being held on to, without attacking or defending the beliefs. Just lay it out on the table and look at it. That is a metaphor of the way relationship can be used as a helpful tool in awakening.

Friend: So holy relationship is merely a reflection of the Father/Son relationship?

David: Yes, like a miniature of it.

Friend: So in terms of what to do with relationships, the intention is to let each one be a holy relationship?

David: Yes, every one.

Friend: And what if the other person is not aware of all this? It is in my mind anyway, so it is not dependent on the other person, right?

## TRACING BACK UPSETS

David: Every time I am upset, I have projected. Anger is nothing more than an attempt to make someone else feel guilty. Every time I am angry or upset it is an attempt to project the responsibility onto someone else; it is an attempt to play the victim of external happenings again. Seen correctly it is a great opportunity to be grateful for the opportunity to see what is going on in the mind. What am I buying into? What construct or thought-form-association is so important that I am letting it stand between my brother and myself, blocking awareness of my Christ-Self?

If I am offended by a partner, a lover, a friend, a neighbor or someone at work, I am offended in Christ. The Christ is always there in my awareness of it. Whenever I am offended by anything, I have a belief, a grievance, or a block in my own mind that I need to let go of. There is a belief in the mind that I need to see it as just a false idea, something that I do not need to be invested in. There is gratitude for that which the world calls relationship because it allows the opportunity to get in touch with these beliefs and the investment in them. If I get into the ascetic mode and run to the mountains so to speak, to get away from the world and from people, there is still an opportunity to practice mind-watching—to go into the silence and to dis-identify from the thought-forms of the world. But relationship is a great time saver. There is tremendous acceleration when I can use the seeming relationships of this world to help me get in touch with the beliefs and concepts that I am holding on to.

Friend: Is a special hate relationship simply looking at that as an attack instead of as an opportunity? Isn't a special hate relationship one in which I feel I have something to lose and something to protect and defend against attack, instead of seeing it as an opportunity to get in touch with the constructs that I am invested in?

## SPECIAL RELATIONSHIPS

David: Special love relationships are really just a masked form of hatred. It is not as if special hate is an attack and special love in some way is not; it is just a different form. The special love relationship is very deceptive because it seems to be that you are complimenting me, that you are agreeing with my views. You are bringing me pleasure. I love having you around in the special love relationship because you are fulfilling needs. But, because you are literally my substitute for God, the flipside is always *Watch out if you stop agreeing with me! You had better not stop providing me with what I need, change from what you have done in the past, or deviate in any way.* For then the wrath of the ego comes up and breaks through, even in the special love relationships; the flipside of a compliment is always a rejection. Both are unreal. The self that is being complimented is a construct as well. When you start to see that they are just two different forms of the same thing, you can withdraw from investing in that.

*The Urantia Book, Part IV* addresses this in several places. The apostles describe Jesus as being very caring and compassionate yet without flattery. In this world compassion and flattery are associated; compliments are associated with caring. This is not true empathy. This is not true caring in the metaphysical sense. True caring is to look beyond appearance and to remember and accept others for who they are, not to buy in at all to behavior or what they say or do not say.

Friend: Not to buy into any of the appearances?

David: Exactly. Because the appearances are the construct; the appearances are the veil.

Friend: So to even compliment someone on appearance is to reinforce the construct? Complimenting you reinforces in my mind that you are what you appear to be, and therefore I am what I appear to be?

David: Yes, which is the body–a person in a world of guilt.

Friend: That is a whole new way of looking at compliments isn't it?

## GOING BEYOND APPEARANCES

David: It is very subtle. When you study the masters, you see they have such compassion and caring; they are very concerned with their pupils' thoughts and beliefs and are constantly pointing those things out in a very gentle way. There can be certain traits that are reflections of holy relationship, reflections of purity of thought that you can rejoice in with one another but when we say "compliment," we are really focusing on the ego's attempt to compliment the body or particular skills that are associated with the body, in order to raise them up as being important. To tell someone that they have improved and are now a better self than before still maintains the construct. It does not get beyond it.

Friend: That is a reason not to adorn the body in a way that draws attention to it, right? It is that very thing of adding reality or importance to what is just a body.

David: Yes, to make something of nothing. It is not often seen that way but if God is Spirit and Christ is Spirit and the body is nothing, then when the mind attempts to make important that which is non-existent we must obviously have a major identity deception going on. The construct is relinquished by withdrawing the investment in appearances and focusing the mind's attention on healing or the One Intent – which you can call forgiveness, or the miracle. The construct is laid aside; it is outgrown.

Friend: Why would a mind that sees the body as nothing want to put anything towards *nothing*? Why would it want to spend time and energy in dolling up and beautifying *nothing*?

David: It would only want to do that if it believed it *was* that thing – that the body was its chosen home and that it could actually make that home better. It is not that you have to sacrifice or become an ascetic. Once you start to get the metaphysics you begin to see that changes in form flow automatically from changes in perception and thinking. It is not the other way around.

## RETRANSLATING APPEARANCES

Friend: So trying to change the form when the mind hasn't been changed would feel like sacrifice, or deprivation?

David: Yes, part of the mind will try to go through with it if there is a belief that at some level it has a value, and there is a conflict in the mind when the mind is split like that.

Friend: There's where resentment would come in?

David: Yes, like a sense of coercion. *I'm doing this for God. I'm doing this because Jesus tells me I have to.* Jesus wants us to start thinking like him; then the behavior will automatically follow from the thoughts. The thought or the mind level is the only place where true change can take place. Changing the form per se, as if it was possible to just change form, is like changing constructs and still holding the belief in the construct in mind. It does not solve anything.

Friend: I can notice what goes on at a form level and use that to start seeing the beliefs in my mind. I can notice how much time I spend coloring my hair or whatever I do that pampers or beautifies the body. I can just notice that I have placed value in the body and use that as a signal to go back in the mind and look at what is really going on; what is the construct that is held in place that would have me put that kind of mind energy toward a body?

David: What is it *for*? What is all the dolling up for? When you really ask a fundamental question like that you can get a sense of the construct; those actions are the mind asking the body to play out fantasies that seem to reinforce that it *is* a body. The mind can have fantasies of pleasure, pain, attack, defense, etc., but the mind cannot truly attack. If the mind could attack then guilt would be justified.

Friend: And the separation could have happened, I guess, in that framework?

David: Yes. The attack thoughts that Jesus talks about in the Course are in the wrong mind. For example, lesson 338, "I am affected only by my thoughts," or lesson 26, "My attack thoughts are attacking my invulnerability." These are part of the split mind.

## HEALING AND MIND-WATCHING

Friend: They are part of the construct that we are talking about.

David: They are, and the healing comes from pulling back and dis-identifying – from being able to watch those attack thoughts without horror. Instead of being horrible, terrifying attack thoughts, they are just *unreal* thoughts! Therefore the horror is gone. From the right mind these thoughts are not horrifying because it is known they are unreal. The Holy Spirit does not buy into the false beliefs. He is anchored in the true identity of the Son and the Source.

So with relationships it comes back to the mind-watching. It is about watching and noticing my feelings and reactions. Those are my trigger points, those are my clues offering a gateway to go in and question the self-concept, false beliefs and associations. There is a moment by moment golden opportunity if one can watch one's feelings and have a willingness to see the world differently, to withdraw the meanings that have been read into the perceptions and the world.

Friend: That seems to be accelerated in a so-called relationship with someone that does not always see eye-to-eye with me. Of course even if we do seem to be on the same page, there is still all the stuff that comes up around intimacy. The acceleration does not have to come about through being in a so-called relationship with someone that I am at odds with.

David: Special love relationships and special hate relationships are just flipsides of the desire to see the split – good guys/bad guys, desirable friends/undesirable friends. It comes back to the mind wanting to see the split out in the world. There really is no difference. True relationship is a state of mind. It is not dependent on *anything* external. And when we speak about special love and special hate relationships, these are metaphors as well for the trick that the mind is trying to do, as if it knows what love is. Attraction and attachment are words that might be more suitable to love as this world sees it.

Friend: And fantasy.

David: Yes. *Meet my needs.*

Friend: It is a humbling thought to remember that I do not really know what love is and that anything I have thought has been love in this world has not been it.

David: An open mind can begin to get a glimmer. The relinquishment of judgment leads to a change in perception, to a more stabilized perception as well as to feelings of peace, wholeness, joy and completion. The seeking ends.

Friend: When I acknowledge that I do not know what I am looking for and that I probably wouldn't recognize it if I saw it, then I guess it is kind of pointless to keep seeking.

## True Happiness – the Light Within

David: Even the deceived mind can say that it is looking for love and happiness but the question is *where* it is looking. The deceived mind counsels the ego, which looks out in the world, or in "the darkened glass" as it says in Corinthians. So the mind is looking for happiness but it is looking outward to the projection to find it, whereas inward is where it can be found. The light in the mind is where it is; the false beliefs, concepts and constructs are covering over the light in the mind, covering over the love and completion that is in the mind.

Friend: So removing the obstacles to that love means removing those constructs from my mind?

David: Or dis-identifying from those constructs.

Friend: Yes, recognizing they are just constructs. There is nothing really to remove, it is just about recognizing that constructs is all that they are – like you say, not identifying with them but rather disregarding them.

David: Yes, this is not a process of destroying the false or destroying the evil. It is a matter of not being fooled, not believing that the false is true, not believing that the unreal is real. Truth is recognition, but you have to be able to identify the false as false before you can experience that recognition. It is really a sorting out of thoughts that the Holy Spirit is helping the mind with; false thoughts are no longer valued or invested in. They begin to fade.

Friend: Because they are recognized for what they are?

David: Yes! Life just becomes One Big Holy Encounter.

## MULTIPLICITY OF IMAGES
## AND THE DECEIVED MIND

David: There is an inward direction to stepping out of the maze of time and space. The inner voice, the intuition, the Holy Spirit keeps guiding the mind to let go of the limited constructs. There is a sorting out of the false from the true, helping the mind to stay at the mind level. It is not about raising the body, the world and attack thoughts to the level of mind. It is about seeing projection as a projection. Projection can feel like a hall of mirrors; the fragmentation and the splitting just seem to go on and on and on. That is the way that the mind deceives itself.

Television is a good example of the projected world mirroring images. It seems like the image that is the person, watches other images on the screen. The projection continues to fragment and splinter. It is this fragmentation of images that seems to be the multiplicity of the world. More and more images are produced in television and advertising. There is tremendous variety, more things to see and do – a multiplication of images – when in fact it is all just part of the construct. A hundred times zero or a thousand times zero is still zero! Things are not getting worse in the world. Things are not getting better in the world. The world is the world.

There is a way of seeing the entire world as a fabric. Stepping back from ordering of thoughts and from judgment literally releases the mind from its belief in littleness. The television is just neutral in the sense that it can be used by the trained mind, by the Holy Spirit, to help see the false as false – to not buy into particular images. To the untrained mind these images reinforce the belief in separation and fragmentation. To the untrained mind the learning of the world continues with television. The perceptions and fragmentations are reinforced as being real; the beliefs continue to be reinforced as being real.

Because the projections and images are reinforced, and are reinforcing the beliefs in the mind, it can be very helpful to take time to sit and talk with children who watch television a lot, asking, "What does that mean to you?" You can use the conversation and whatever is on the screen as a teaching/learning device. Talk about the meaning that is given and get into a discussion of values and the deeper levels of the mind.

Friend: That is when the Holy Spirit is at work, using the images as part of training the mind towards greater discernment of sorting out the true from the false.

David: And if one does not have a lot of time to sit down and talk with a child who is watching TV, it can be helpful to very carefully select programs that are reinforcing more helpful values as well as to limit television when it is unsupervised or when there is no one to really discuss and go into the different meanings with.

Television is an arena that a lot of people have questions about. It can seem to be very seductive. Sitting there and watching the images seems to present a picture of reality, but has nothing to do with reality in the ultimate sense. Like everything else, it can be used as a symbol by the Holy Spirit to undo the false concepts, or it can be used by the ego for the purpose of reinforcing belief in fragmentation, victims and victimizers. The ego can be very drawn to the fighting and the battles because they reinforce the belief in competition. Seen differently, by a trained mind, the same images are simply seen as a call for help and, in the ultimate sense, as unreal. They can be used as a tool for release. It is helpful to look at the intention in the mind, to ask yourself, "What is it for, for me? If I am trying to get something from it, what is it that makes me value one program over another?" It is about discerning between the Holy Spirit's and the ego's purpose.

Body identification takes many different forms in the world. Whether through fashion, body building, or dieting, etc., a standardized form of beauty is sought after. The important thing is to look at the purpose. The ego emphasizes the form identity because that identification is what protects it from the light in the mind. This substitute is what protects the belief in separation. It tells the mind that the body is its chosen home, even though it is not a very good home for the mind in the sense that it is fallible and vulnerable. The intention is to pull back away from thinking that you can see the ego in anything or anywhere. Some people might say that a shopping mall for instance, with its emphasis on all the different services made available to the body, is like the temple of the ego. You could say that metaphorically, but ultimately it is important to remember that the desires for the things of the world are *in the mind*.

Friend: Not in the shopping mall.

David: Not in the shopping mall. To see it there is level confusion. Level confusion "always entails the belief that what is amiss on one level can adversely affect another … all mistakes must be corrected at the level on which they occur." (T-2.IV.2) The mistake occurs in the mind.

## THE BODY AS A COMMUNICATION DEVICE

David: It is one thing to call the body unreal or *nothing* but the ego would say that the body is evil. The first step is to see that the body can be used by the Holy Spirit for the Holy Spirit's purpose. In that sense and in that sense only is the body a "temple," as some people have called it. This has nothing to do with the body in and of itself; it has to do with the intention or the purpose in mind. We could say that a body used solely for communication is a body used by the Holy Spirit.

Friend: That brings us to the topic of communication. Communication is not necessarily what I have been educated to believe it is. Communication does not have to include two bodies. Communication happens at a mind level and that is the *only* place where it happens. So why do I need a body to communicate if it only happens at the mind level?

David: Every mind that seems to believe in the world of separation and the body believes that communication is limited. Communion, or mind communication, or you might even call it telepathy, has been blocked and pushed out of awareness. The body has literally been imposed as a limit on communication. In this world it appears that if two bodies are not together, communication is limited. In other words, they cannot talk to one another unless they use a telephone or some kind of material aid for communication.

In the ultimate sense we are back to the belief—the body is believed in and the world is believed in. But the world was made as a *limit* on communication. The world was made to defend against communication. The Holy Spirit is our communication link with the Father; the world was made to cover that over. The Holy Spirit works with the lower mind, helping it to let go of its beliefs in the world. As it does, it appears as if the powers of the mind are gradually returned. Telepathy, clairvoyance and intuition seem to be more prevalent in the mind when actually the mind is simply returning to its natural condition. These are not supernatural powers that rare individuals can develop. These are very natural communication mechanisms.

Friend: So the communication is always there and has always been there, but it is covered over, blocking awareness of it?

David: It is the strong investment in the body that does this. The body is the chosen home of the deceived mind. It uses the body for pride, pleasure and attack—all purposes that constrain communication. The Holy Spirit's sole purpose or function for the body is communication

Friend: Before we get into pride, pleasure and attack, could we review the Holy Spirit's use for the body? If communication is solely at a mind level, why have a body to be used for communication? I think what I hear you saying is, "As long as the mind believes in the body then the Holy Spirit uses that body for communication." It is only the belief in the body that has the body entering into the communication at all. Without that belief there would be full, total awareness of where communication is already, at the mind level?

David: Yes. There are no bodies in the holy instant. Revelation is beyond bodies. It is direct communication from God to God's Creation. When the mind gives up its false ideas, false beliefs and judgments it is drawn into the holy instant where communication is completely restored. The Holy Spirit will reach a mind that is deceived in whatever way that He can. Bodies are symbols; the Holy Spirit can come through the voice of a friend, as well as through a sign on a billboard or in a song lyric and so on. There are many ways and many forms for reaching the mind. The Holy Spirit uses symbols to reach the deceived mind because the deceived mind believes in symbols. Metaphorically, as we move forward in this and get clearer we are able to line up with the Holy Spirit's purpose; we are asked to reach our brothers who believe in the world, in time and separation.

We are asked to reach them using symbols that they can hear and understand. Jesus is a great example of that. He spoke in parables to the masses but he spoke of higher ideals and concepts when he spoke to the apostles and the disciples who had the ears to hear. In both cases the Holy Spirit was speaking through him using symbols the mind can grasp. We also have examples of Jesus going off into the silence, into communion with the Father. We have a range of communication starting with words, which are still very crude, but as the mind lets go of the beliefs we come back into wordless communion.

Friend: The Holy Spirit uses everything within the illusion as symbols, right?

David: Yes, though when we say that the Holy Spirit uses the symbols of the world some might think that the Holy Spirit is working in the world.

Friend: You mean they might think the Holy Spirit is external to the mind, working in the world?

## SYMBOLS AND THE
## CORRECTION OF PERCEPTION

David: That is a common idea or belief for a mind that believes it is in the world, for a mind that has no conception of the inner life. It is so convinced about the concrete and the specific that it needs specific symbols. Those symbols can take many forms. There can be appearances by angels, voices, near-death experiences, etc. We need to pull it back and see that the Holy Spirit is the abstract light in the mind and that He literally is working with the lower mind, with the beliefs. When the mind starts to open up to the light and begins to let go of beliefs in the limiting concepts that it has placed on itself, then symbols appear that are perceived by the mind. It can appear as if there is something external that is tinkering with the world, creating a parking space or providing the rent money just in time. It can seem that these things are happening *to* you, that He is literally "making straight your path, and leaving in your way no stones to trip on, and no obstacles to bar your way." (T-20.IV.8) This is a comforting perception to a mind that still believes in the world, but actually the mind is simply laying aside beliefs and perceiving a world in which things seem to be taken care of.

Friend: So the Holy Spirit is not working in the world within the illusion but working within the mind and then the mind's perception of the world changes accordingly, though it seems that the Holy Spirit had a direct effect on something in the world. Actually the direct effect is merely on the mind that out pictures the world.

David: It is an interpretation, definitely. It can seem as if things are clicking better now whereas before it felt like an uphill battle; in fact, the mind is just opening to and following the guidance.

Friend: Is that an indication of greater receptivity in the mind to being directed?

David: It is symbolic of that.

Friend: Could we go back now to the ego's use for the body: pride, pleasure and attack? Would you address those?

## THE EGO'S USE OF THE BODY

David: Yes, we can take a look at them one by one. Pride is really just a desperate attempt to maintain a belief in personhood, of being an individual person and perceiving other individual persons. It maintains the subject/object split between self and other in the mind. Pride reinforces the split by drawing attention to one's self, one's person, by focusing on accomplishments or physique, pride in one's family, or sports team, or country; pride uses all those things that are considered to be very good.

Friend: Can you talk about spiritual pride?

David: Spiritual pride would be taking pride in what one knows, turning the spiritual journey into a book-learning feat or into a display of abilities; the intention underneath is still to draw attention to the small self, to the personhood. It is a very subtle trap. When people have not let go of their belief in separation in the mind they can use psychic abilities or different types of seeming powers, like telepathy, levitation or psycho-kinesis as a way to draw attention to the "I." *Look what I can do.* It is still the personal "I." It could be about becoming a lecturer or a workshop leader or a renowned healer. It is spiritual pride when it gets personified. It is not doing as Jesus did – pointing to Heaven, saying it is the Father, not I that speaks; "I" am not the source of healing, our Father in Heaven is the Source. He was always pointing to the Father, always taking the second place, identified as the Creation, not the Creator. This is the true humility of a mind that knows what it is, a mind that knows its Source. True humility does not try to take over the king-pin role by placing the personal thought-form-self at the center. It points always to the Father. Spiritual pride takes other forms as well. It can also be about identifying with a particular group or path and projecting superiority; *we know the way. We've got the answer and the rest of the world does not.* It is just another trap among many to still attempt to identify with the small "I," the personal self.

Now let's look at pleasure. Pleasure is part of the world of duality; you can think of pleasure and pain as two extremes. Both are equally unreal and both are defenses against the truth in the sense that they are useful techniques for the ego to use to make the body real, to maintain the body identity. The mind can perceive the flesh or recognize the Spirit. It is one or the other. They are mutually exclusive in awareness. This means that if one is aware of the body and aware of the world, then the recognition of the Spirit is kept from awareness.

The pursuit of pleasure is a distractive device. It anchors the thought that the body is real. It seems to be very attractive; this is what the Course refers to as the attraction of guilt. The deceived mind does not see. It does not equate guilt and pleasure. Pleasure is seen as something very desirable, something to be sought after, and something good. A lot of times you will hear things

65

like, "God wants you to enjoy yourself. Take part in the menus of the world. Enjoy the variety and many spices and pleasures of the world. God wants you to enjoy yourself." But, from the metaphysical perspective, first of all God is Spirit. God does not know about the physical projected world. God only knows His Creation, which is the Son, and He knows him as perfect. This is a pure, abstract, infinite relationship that has nothing to do with form in any way. Basically the mind is unaware that the pursuit of pleasure and the avoidance of pain are the same; by pursuing pleasure one is also pursuing pain.

Friend: And both of them act as substitutes for God?

David: Yes. We talked about the pursuit of wealth in this world as well as the belief in poverty and lack, in a material sense. There are many forms of the same kind of split, the same guise. The poor yearn for more possessions, for an easier life so to speak, and those who are supposedly living the good life still feel pain, anguish and depression. The mind is still seeking for happiness in the world; it is just seeking in the wrong place! Peace and contentment and happiness are found in the mind that has let go of false beliefs.

Attack is something that is very important as a defense against the truth. Attack is a witness that separation has occurred. To truly see that separation is impossible seems to be at odds with what the body's eyes see. As one looks around the world through the ego's distorted perception attack is seen in many different forms. There are arguments, verbal attacks, physical attacks, weapons, knives, bombs, etc. There seems to be a world where attack is the common experience, but the mind cannot attack. The mind is abstract. The mind is one. It can only make up body fantasies where attack seems to be real. Ego uses the body for attack. It is a fantasy of attack and it definitely makes guilt seem real. If attack is perceived as real, then guilt is justified, and if guilt is justified, how can one be wholly innocent? How can one be the holy innocent child of God as one was Created?

Friend: You are saying it is fantasy because it is all pretend? It is all made up?

David: It is all made up and it is just on the screen. The deceived mind wants to see the conflict not in the mind but in the world! Under the ego's counsel, the mind will look for conflict in the world. This is not to say that war or sports or verbal abuse per se are bad. It is not to say that anything is evil; it is the interpretation that has to be looked at. A healed mind can calmly look upon any sight in the world. The body's eyes will still report to the mind changes in circumstances and in symptoms, etc., but the healed mind just puts them all into one category and that is, *they are unreal!* You have to really have a clear metaphysical idea of why this is so, of why sickness must be impossible or why competition cannot be, why there cannot be victims and victimizers in the world. One must have a very clear idea that *it is all in the mind*. It all comes down to that subject/object split.

Friend: So it is because it is all unreal that the Course says that the world is neutral, neither good nor bad, that it all has to do with how the mind looks upon it. It is all just a projection of the picture in your mind.

David: To the Holy Spirit the world is neutral. Remember, it is just a screen. It is just a projection, symbols the Holy Spirit can use for His purpose. To the deceived mind, the world is not neutral because it has chosen to order the thoughts that make up the world in a configuration or a construct that make it seem real, so real that the mind thinks it is a figure in the world instead of the one dreaming it. It is a little dream figure, a person that has

67

things to do and a life to defend! To the deceived mind, the world is anything but neutral; it has judged and ordered it.

Friend: It is always good or bad, or something in between. It is always something, never neutral.

David: Right, to the deceived mind. Now the miracle is like a glimpse, a remembering of the neutrality, of the unreality of the world. There is a sense of easiness and of gentle watching because the mind is seen to be the dreamer. There is detachment in the miracle; there has been a choice to give the mind over to the Holy Spirit, to align with the right mind. There is a stepping back from trying to control what is happening on the screen and a willingness to look upon things with gentle detachment, without judging them.

Friend: Would you talk about judgment a little bit? Isn't it the attempt to control what is on the screen, by judging everything that seems to pass before these eyes?

## THE HIERARCHY OF ILLUSION – JUDGMENT AND THE ORDERING OF THOUGHTS

David: Judgment as used in more common terminology is associated with condemnation, put-downs, and a kind of superior/inferior dynamic. That is the common usage. *I've got to quit criticizing, let go of my grievances, etc.* Judgment goes much deeper than that. If we follow that idea through, we could say judgment is to make unequal. It makes what is equal appear unequal. The Sonship is one; a metaphor for this world is that everyone, or every brother, is equal. When we bring it back to the deeper levels we see that ordering of thoughts is the same as judgment. A condemnation or a criticism is a kind of ordering or judging of "better than thou," but on a more subtle level we see that the entire world is nothing more than a projection of thoughts. "My thoughts are images that I have made." (W-15) It is the ordering of thoughts that maintains the illusion of the reality of the world.

Friend: So if any kind of ranking in my mind is an ordering of thoughts, a judgment, then it does not matter whether what I am looking at is ranked at a one or a ten?

David: Right. "A hierarchy of illusions," (T-23.II.2) is precisely what judgment is. Judgment makes a hierarchy of illusions. If I rate and rank some illusions as more important than other illusions, that blocks the awareness that they are *all* an illusion. They are equally illusory. At the core of judgment is this ranking. In the Manual for Teachers the relinquishment of judgment is called a "necessary condition of salvation." (M-9.2) Also the very first principle of the fifty *Principles of Miracles* is that there is no order of difficulty in miracles. Jesus says that if you could really get the first principle then the rest of the Course would be easy. This is the principle that the ego really defends against. To the ego, there is enormous order of difficulty. In following the spiritual path one tries to see the Christ in everyone by not ordering and judging people, situations and events. This is precisely what the ego is holding on to. That is its bread and butter.

Friend: Is it that very ordering that holds the world intact for the ego, for the deceived mind?

David: Yes. I have used the example of going to a restaurant that you have gone to a number of times. Say you like their cherry cheesecake; this time when you go in and order your cherry cheesecake the waiter says, "I'm sorry, we are out of cherry cheesecake." The reason you have an experience of disappointment or deprivation is the ordering of thoughts. The cherry cheesecake was raised up and became part of the construct, of the concept, of the person; *I like cherry cheesecake.* It is not that you have to go around judging or condemning vanilla ice cream, but if it is ranked lower than the cherry cheesecake there is an order of preferences that is part of the hierarchy of illusions. The self-concept is literally a construct of ordered thoughts. *I like sunny days more than rainy days; I like warm climates more than cool climates; I like to drive a Mercury as opposed to a Jaguar; I like women who have long dark hair as opposed to blondes; I like these television shows better than those.* You see how it goes on and on and on. It is all part of the ordering and the ranking. This is the judgment that holds the world up, the stilts underneath the projection of the world. If you took the stilts away then the world would collapse. It would fade away.

Friend: So having preferences is the same as ordering one's thoughts? If I am ordering or ranking my thoughts, then I've got preferences?

David: That could seem to be very overwhelming. It can be tempting to think it is too big of a job. Preferences run so deep; they run right down to the core of the personhood-idea. For every person there seems to be an enormous number of preferences and likes and dislikes. It is even encouraged to be unique, to be an individual and to have your own opinions.

Friend: To know what you like and to know what you want and what you don't want.

David: At this point we could say that it is truly important to focus on forgiveness and focus on that one intent. Focus on watching the thoughts and slowly pulling away from investing in them. Allow the joy of following the Holy Spirit as these thoughts become unordered, undone so to speak. The constructed order becomes undone. This is a process of following the joy of connecting. The joy that comes from not judging is so strong and intense that the preferences fade away.

When you hear that these preferences are all part of the ego concept there can be a temptation to try to decide this instant to stop having any preferences. There can be some level confusion where you are trying to change on the level of form, like quitting smoking or drinking coffee, without having the mind shift on the inside, without following the joy. By following the joy the mind allows these preferences and desires to fade away as it gets focused on its one function. Without that focus the level confusion will creep in; you will just be changing behaviors without changing the mind – without letting go of the false beliefs.

The ego is *for* something that is nothing and it has the illusion of being a genius. It seems to have made up a world – a giant cosmos apart from Spirit and apart from abstract union. The world it made up seems to have great diversity, a great variety of skills, choices and menus to choose from. In the sense of projection we now have TVs, camcorders and DVDs; it is like movies within movies. The movie of the world is one movie and within that movie we have another projection. The fragmentation just continues on into these seeming smaller pieces.

One thing that the ego has tried to come up with as an answer to Heaven is immortality, which it never has and never will be able to mimic or create. Immortality is an attribute of God, of Creation and the ego is a defense against that. The ego is literally a puff of nothingness that did not come from God and is not immortal. The ego seemed to have a beginning and it will seem to have an end, all within the fabric or the framework of the dream. The fact that the ego never has and never will be able to develop immortality does not stop it from at least having the idea of immortality, the idea that the body can be made to live forever. The body is form; form and Spirit have no reconciliation, no meeting point. One Spirit exists. Form, time and space do not.

Friend: And the very nature of form is that it is finite, that it is not eternal and cannot therefore be immortal.

David: Yes, it has boundaries. Every form has boundaries and limits. God and Creation do not.

Friend: I remember something I heard about this person Babaji in India. He seemed to be proof that the body is immortal. It seemed that he had been around for periods of time and then he would dematerialize. He would not be around for other periods of time and then he would rematerialize and stay for a while and then dematerialize and so on. I suppose it has been going on for quite some time now. That seemed to be prove that we do not have to die, that the body can be immortal if it is held in the mind that way.

## REACHING THE DECEIVED MIND THROUGH SYMBOLS

David: Seeing a body or a vision is still perception, however in this scenario the body seems to come and go. Your example can be a symbol–for many, a very comforting symbol. It can be a symbol of teaching. The thoughts of those who have completely laid aside the body are always available to the deceived mind, as an aid. The vision may appear from time to time if that is helpful. The Holy Spirit can reach the deceived mind in many ways and these are nothing more than symbols. For example, the seeing of the Virgin Mary in the Catholic tradition over in Medjugorje is another example of a vision that can be helpful. But they are still perceptions.

Friend: So it is still perceptual and unreal but it is helpful; it is reaching the mind where it is?

David: Yes. The error would be to make the connection that you made, that a body could be immortal just because it seems that it has been around for so long a time. Knowledge or the Kingdom of Heaven is purely abstract. It is light. It is not a light like the body's eyes see but a light of understanding and wisdom. Darkness is a metaphor for ignorance or the blockage of the awareness of that light. However pure, however stabilized the perception becomes it is still not knowledge. It is not the abstract Kingdom. It is still perceptual and temporary and will not last.

## THE IMPOSSIBILITY OF ATTACK AND THE ILLUSION OF SICKNESS

To finish up on the point about the ego's uses for the body, of pride, pleasure and attack; they are all the same. You could say that pride and pleasure are seeming forms of attack. Ego is an attack thought, an attack on the Christ within the mind that believes it is an ego. Even though the ego has no basis in reality, it is given reality by the mind's acceptance of that thought. To the mind it seems real. And all the uses of the body, whether we talk about pride in the personal self or pleasure and pain, etc., they are all the attraction of guilt. It is all a way of concealing the belief in separation and keeping the mind distracted on the screen. In that sense they are all attack thoughts. The uses that the ego has for the body are all part of attack thoughts.

Now, if we pull it back to the right mind, these thoughts are unreal thoughts; the mind cannot attack. Even the thoughts that are called attack thoughts are unreal. They have not come from the mind of God. They do not exist. Only thoughts that come from God have existence.

Friend: So to speak of attack thoughts is just a manner of speaking?

David: Yes, they are unreal. A mind that is invested in them is deceived and will experience the hallucination of pain, upset, despair, sorrow, depression, fear, etc., because it has invested in a thought system that does not come from God. The right mind sees that attack is literally impossible. It is not invested in these thoughts. It sees and knows them as false. This is no different than saying that the Holy Spirit sees false ideas as false beliefs and looks to the undefiled altar – the Atonement – and is certain of the Christ. It always looks to the Christ. We are coming full circle to your question about sickness, of why sickness is impossible. It is impossible because the mind cannot attack. The mind is whole and cannot attack. It can make up fantasies. It can direct the body to act out fantasies but it cannot attack.

Friend: And it would have to attack in order for sickness to be reality.

David: The right mind knows that mind cannot attack. The Holy Spirit knows that attack is impossible. The ego is an impossible thought. All of the ego thoughts are impossible and unreal. The right mind is anchored in that. "I am not a body, and my mind cannot attack so I cannot be sick." (W-136) If there is no identification with the body and it is recognized and clearly understood that the mind cannot attack, then, with those two conditions, there is no justification for guilt. There is no attack. There is no body with which to identify with or to attack with, so to speak. Therefore the conditions of peace have been met because the conditions of guilt are no longer in place. If I believe that I am a body and that my mind or body can attack, and I believe that attack is real then guilt must follow; guilt must be justified. You can see how working it back to the right mind and being miracle minded automatically brings about inner peace.

Friend: You mentioned once that in addition to perceiving my body as sick, I can perceive the body of another as sick. You said that in either case it is just an indication that my mind is sick, or mistaken, and needs to be healed. I think that is an important point. I think you can perceive your body as well but still be perceiving sickness in someone else. But I hear you saying that there is really no difference because the perception is mistaken and in need of correction/healing in the mind either way.

## LEVEL CONFUSION

David: We are back to level confusion again. You cannot be in the right mind *and* perceive sickness in the world.

Friend: I can still perceive certain behaviors of the body as it were, so called symptoms of the body, but the healed mind just knows and holds in mind that what the eyes are communicating is not so. It is impossible regardless of what information the eyes and the ears are taking in?

David:

> The body's eyes will continue to see differences. But the mind that has let itself be healed will no longer acknowledge them. There will be those who seem to be "sicker"

75

> than others, and the body's eyes will report their changed
> appearances as before. But the healed mind will put them
> all in one category; they are unreal. (M-8.6)

That should be a hint right there—*into one category.* The split mind has judged, fragmented and ordered the world into different categories; the senses just bring forth witnesses to fill the categories. When the mind ceases to judge, order and make categories for the world, it all gets put into the one category of *unreal.* All is equally seen to be unreal. The illusion of sickness and health are both put into the one category of being unreal.

The body is invulnerable when the healed mind listens to the Holy Spirit's voice, operates in the right mind, and consistently chooses the miracle. The Course tells us that while the mind is following the Voice for God, the body will be used for as long as it is needed and "when its usefulness is done it is laid by." (M-12.5)

It all starts with perception. This is a course in correcting perception and relinquishing judgment.

## MIRACLES AND REVELATION

Friend: So, miracle-mindedness is to just look at whatever the body's eyes see without interpretation? Just to acknowledge what is seen as unreal and impossible, without judging or ranking any of it?

David: Yes. We must also say that we are still speaking in metaphors and using them as stepping stones. We have already said that in revelation and in the holy instant there are no bodies. Perception disappears in revelation. There are no bodies in the light of truth.

Revelation is not normally maintained. If it was, the body would not be retained for long because there would be no need for it. The mind is in such a state of remembrance of the Kingdom that there is no need for a body anymore. The body and the world disappear in that instant, in the Great Rays, in the light of the instant.

Friend: They disappear into the nothingness from which they came. Maybe this is a good time to talk about true perception and the real world, which is as I see it, just that last little step before it all disappears.

David: True perception or the real world is, in a sense, knowledge or love. It is beyond the curriculum of removing the blocks to the awareness of love. True perception/the real world are metaphors for a highly trained mind that has let go of judgment.

Friend: So all those barriers have been removed in the state of true perception or the real world?

David: It is also called the borderland. These are all metaphors for a highly trained mind, the mind that has learned the holy relationship. It has unlearned the ways of the world – the laws of the world. It has learned that it is not governed by those laws. The mind is only governed by the laws of God. The borderland is a metaphor or stepping off point for the mind. Once it reaches this stage it is so close to love; it has gone as high as learning can go. Knowledge is not learned, Knowledge is. The real world, true perception and the borderland are metaphors.

Friend: Is the holy instant another way of describing that? Is that comparable to true perception?

David: The holy instant is described in many ways. It is the gateway, so to speak, to the eternal. While the mind still has attention on the world and sees it as being real in any way, while it still sees a shred of value in the world, it is attempting to bring the past into the holy instant.

> Take this very instant, now, and think of it as all there is of time. Nothing can reach you here out of the past, and it is here that you are completely absolved, completely free and wholly without condemnation. From this holy instant wherein holiness was born again you will go forth in time without fear, and with no sense of change with time. (T-15.I.9)

When the mind truly lets go of everything else, it lets go into the holy instant. In that sense it is the gateway to eternity. There is an eternal aspect of the Holy Spirit that the Course says will remain with you always in Heaven. You could make an analogy between the Holy Spirit and the holy instant, while the miracle is described more as perceptual.

Friend: So there is a perceptual component in the real world and true perception but not in the holy instant?

David: When you experience the holy instant, there are no bodies. It is more analogous to revelation, to the Great Rays. Here we are using terms again but the holy instant is an *experience*. A miracle is an experience. To be in the right mind is an experience. These are just words that are tools for the mind to use to meet it where it believes it is, as a springboard to this experience.

You cannot prepare for the holy instant. That might feel like a mind-blowing concept. You may wonder why you are putting so many hours into the study of the Course seemingly preparing your mind for something that cannot be prepared for! "You cannot prepare for it without placing it in the future." (T-18.VII.4) To prepare for something is to put it into the future and the holy instant is now. It is this instant, this present. There is a trap in the ideas of *becoming* and *preparing for*; that all has to be laid aside as well.

Friend: All that's required for the holy instant is the desire and the willingness to experience it?

David: A very single-minded, whole-hearted desire – the desire for nothing else. Here is a summary of some of the things we have been talking about; it is laid out very clearly in the *I Need Do Nothing* section:

> You still have too much faith in the body as a source of strength. What plans do you make that do not involve its comfort or protection or enjoyment in some way? This makes the body an end and not a means in your interpretation, and this always means you still find sin attractive. No one accepts Atonement for himself who still accepts sin as his goal. You have thus not met your *one* responsibility. Atonement is not welcomed by those who prefer pain and destruction.

> There is one thing that you have never done; you have not utterly forgotten the body. It has perhaps faded at times from your sight, but it has not yet completely disappeared. You are not asked to let this happen for more than an instant, yet it is in this instant that the miracle of Atonement happens. Afterwards you will see the body again, but never quite the same. And every instant that you spend without awareness of it gives you a different view of it when you return.

> At no single instant does the body exist at all. It is always remembered or anticipated, but never experienced just *now*. Only its past and future make it seem real. Time

controls it entirely, for sin is never wholly in the present. In any single instant the attraction of guilt would be experienced as pain and nothing else, and would be avoided. It has no attraction *now*. Its whole attraction is imaginary, and therefore must be thought of in the past or in the future.

It is impossible to accept the holy instant without reservation unless, just for an instant, you are willing to see no past or future. You cannot prepare for it without placing it in the future. (T-18.VII.1-4)

Friend: That was your very point, wasn't it?

David: Yes. If we place the holy instant – the Atonement – in the future, it is still a concept; it is still feared and there is still a gap. "Release is given you the instant you desire it." (T-18. VII.4) Desire is the key thing and as I said, it needs to be wholehearted desire.

"Many have spent a lifetime in preparation, and have indeed achieved their instants of success." (T-18.VII.4) He is speaking on the level of the world, on the level of the Course where you have stages in the development of trust. This definitely seems to be preparation. The mind goes through stages. It seems to be that judgment is relinquished step by step. It seems that forgiveness involves steps and that time involves intervals that in reality do not exist. The miracle is like a time collapse, the collapse of a time interval which is still within the framework of the dream. But in the ultimate sense of it, it was a gentle correction, a gentle plan of awakening from the belief in separation that involves intervals that in reality do not exist. The preparation we are talking about in this sense is still within the world's framework.

If we skip down we come to an interesting set of sentences:

> To do anything involves the body. And if you recognize you need do nothing, you have withdrawn the body's value from your mind. Here is the quick and open door through which you slip past centuries of effort, and escape from time. This is the way in which sin loses all attraction *right now*. For here is time denied, and past and future gone. Who needs do nothing has no need for time. (T-18.VII.7)

On the next page we come back to the idea of the body. We have talked about the body as being a limit on communication. The Holy Spirit can still use the body as a symbol and words as a crude kind of a stepping stone towards that leaping-off point where the mind is returned to Communication with the Father, or Communion. This section here really summarizes and anchors what we have been talking about:

> It is only the awareness of the body that makes love seem limited. For the body *is* a limit on love. The belief in limited love was its origin and it was made to limit the unlimited. Think not that this is merely allegorical, for it was made to limit *you*. Can you who see yourself within a body know yourself as an idea? (T-18.VIII.1)

An idea, of course, is abstract. The idea here is the Christ, the Son of God. It is an idea in the Mind of God. Ideas leave not their source; the idea of Christ has never left its Source, which is the Mind of God.

> Everything you recognize you identify with externals, something outside itself. You cannot even think of God without a body, or in some form you think you recognize. (T-18.VIII.1)

This relates to our talk about the construct, the self-concept; everything that is identified with externally is part of that construct.

## DISSOLVING THE PROJECTED GOD

David: *Everything* you are identified with externally is part of that construct – personhood, world, country, sexuality; male/female, skills, attributes, etc.

Friend: Even my idea of God is just part of a construct?

David: The deceived mind has a projected God. It can be the anthropomorphic God of the Old Testament for example; a God that is angry and punitive at times, and loving at other times. This is a projected God, a God of the future, a God that will someday save mankind. It is like the mind has a hologram of time and space around it, to protect it from love; it has to give up its investment and belief in the hologram before it can spring into awareness.

Friend: So it even has to give up its belief in God?

David: Yes, the belief in a projected God.

Friend: And that *is* the belief the mind holds, a belief in a projected God? So part of the undoing is giving up the belief in God as the deceived mind holds it.

## HOLD ONTO NOTHING

David: On the surface it might sound like we are getting into blasphemy here. Someone might think we are telling them to give up their belief in God. We can use a passage from lesson 189 in the Workbook: "Simply do this: Be still, and lay aside all thoughts of what you are and what God is." (W-189.7) There it is, very clearly stated in *A Course in Miracles* – lay aside *all* thoughts about what you are and what God is.

> Empty your mind of everything it thinks is either true or false, or good or bad, of every thought it judges worthy, and of all the ideas of which it is ashamed. Hold on to nothing." (W-189.7)

This relates to the passage from *The Little Garden* in the Text: "Everything you recognize you identify with externals, something outside itself." (T-18.VIII.1) There *is* nothing outside the Son of God. There is nothing other than God and Creation and the Son's Creations; abstract light and infinity is truth. Truth has existence and nothing else does. That rules out the cosmos!

> The body cannot know and while you limit your awareness to its tiny senses, you will not see the grandeur that surrounds you. God cannot come into a body, nor can you join Him there. (T-18.VIII.2)

That rules out the idea of the immortality of the body.

> Limits on love will always seem to shut Him out, and keep you apart from Him. The body is a tiny fence around a little part of a glorious and complete idea. It draws a circle, infinitely small, around a very little segment of Heaven, splintered from the whole, proclaiming that within it is your kingdom where God can enter not. (T-18.VIII.2)

As we close this reading from the Course, we can jump to the end of next page: "Do not accept this little fenced-off aspect as yourself." (T-18.VIII.7)

And the beginning of the next paragraph: "Love knows no bodies, and reaches to everything created like itself. Its total lack of limit *is* its meaning." (T-18.VIII.8)

This paints a picture for us of the abstractness, of the infinite nature of love, and of God. It really makes it clear that there is no reconciliation between the body, the world, and God. God did not create the body and God did not create the world. They are temporal, fleeting, changing and therefore in the ultimate sense have no existence; what God Creates is eternal, changeless and limitless.

Friend: And only what God Created exists.

David: Yes.

## CREATION AND CREATIVITY

Friend: You made some references to the creations of the Son of God. Let's talk about "my" creations. That comes up repeatedly in the Course and it seems pretty vague to me. Is that because the creations are *abstract* and not known to the deceived mind? Is it only when the deceived mind is no longer deceived that the creations will be recognized and experienced?

David: An awakened mind that knows what Creation is and knows what Creativity is, is aware of that which has come from its extension.

Friend: So creativity has nothing to do with what might be

thought of as creativity in terms of a very creative, artistic, imaginative mind that expresses itself?

David: Creativity has absolutely nothing to do with imagination. In a sense, one could say that the Course is a very creative expression – pages and pages of poetic Shakespearian blank verse with iambic pentameter. It points to and is expressive of something much higher. This is often the sense of creativity in this world, but creation and true creativity have nothing at all to do with the symbols and the forms and images of the world. That is imagination. Creation involves extension, Spirit begetting Spirit. There is increase involved but not a quantifiable increase. It is not like in this world, one, two, three, four and more, in a quantifiable sense, but we read that the Kingdom of Heaven, God and His Creations, are always increasing.

Friend: What does "increase but not in a quantifiable sense" mean?

David: Well, it is expansive yet without the concept of size. It is difficult to conceptualize. Revelation is not transferable in a conceptual sense in terms of words, which is precisely the point. We use words and concepts to try to convey it but revelation is an experience beyond concepts. Creation and Creativity can be experienced but they are not transferable in the conceptual sense. The experience cannot be transferred through words. It is a highly personal experience as the Course talks about in the early part of the text. Even to attempt to explain these things is missing the mark.

Jesus has a kind of theoretical take on it in the Text, describing Creations as being extensions. We can talk about cause and effect; God is the Cause and God's Creation – Christ – is His Effect. And the Son has Creative ability and is a co-Creator in the sense of having the power of God and having the ability to extend it. Creation is to extend, to increase. The Creations are the Effect of the Son of God.

Friend: Even though it seems that I am not recognizing what those Creations are and I can't talk about them, what still comes through for me in various places in the Course is that there is great joy associated with them.

David: Yes. Within the framework of the dream a veil is drawn between my Creations and my awareness of my Creations. When the veil is lifted there is full awareness; there is a state of being *one with* my Creations.

Friend: Are there things in the world that in some way reflect my Creations?

David: The things in the world are part of the veil and literally *block* the awareness of Creation. The deceived mind projects out separate things that are seen as separate and apart from the fabric: trees, caterpillars, birds, butterflies, bears, rainbows, bodies and so on. That is the veil. That is perception.

Creations are part of an experience of union that is known when the veil is lifted. There is nothing in the world that can reflect this. If we said that butterflies, for example, are reflections of my Creations, or of God or Heaven, we are back to the idea of seeing God in specifics, in the world—which cannot be since "God knows not form." (T-30.III.4)

"God is in everything I see." (W-29) "God is in everything I see because God is in my mind." (W-30) This is about a way of looking; it is about the vision of the Holy Spirit which does not order the world into a hierarchy of illusions. It is vision that sees the false as false. Instead of separate objects there is just a blanket of forgiveness covering all of the seeming perceived, separate objects of the world. To relate back to our discussion about ending the duality of subject and object – from the state of unity or true perception which the Holy Spirit is – there is the reflection of love. It still involves perception so it is not love itself, but it is a new purpose given to the projected world.

Friend: So it is that experience of unity, of oneness, that is a reflection? Is it like the oneness that comes through in a holy relationship that can be said to be a reflection of the only oneness that there is?

David: Yes. The holy relationship in this world is a learning accomplishment. It is about unlearning false ideas and beliefs and learning true perception. In that sense it is a reflection of unity, of oneness. But in the ultimate sense union, or oneness, is abstract. It is knowledge or Heaven. Any time we speak of the perceptual realm we can speak only of the reflection of love or the reflection of union.

Friend: We are always somewhat removed from the whole realm of revelation when we are talking about anything that has a perceptual component in it. Is that what you're saying?

David: Words just don't even come close to it. In the Workbook Jesus says, "We say 'God is' and then cease to speak." (W-169.5) That is a metaphor for a state of being that just is. There are other passages where Jesus will begin to speak of something and then just trail off, saying that it cannot be spoken of.

There is work to be done to look at the false ideas and concepts in the mind and dis-identify from them; there is too much work to do along those lines to be spending our time trying to describe the indescribable.

# WHAT IS DEATH?

Friend: Our last dialogue began with me asking you to address the illusion of sickness. Since so often it seems that the word sickness and death are joined in the same sentence, I would like to go into a dialogue about that, starting off with the question, "What is death?"

David: What is death? Let's start off by looking at the common usage of the word in the world, which normally would be the death of a body. Whether we are talking about the death of a spouse, a friend, a loved one, a pet, animals, or organic life, death is seen to be in the world. Something is happening. Something that was animated and seemed to be full of movement and life energy seems to suddenly be stagnant and still.

Friend: The breath has left and the heart is no longer beating

David: That gets into definitions. When we define anything in the world we have defined a problem. Death is perceived as a problem. People do not want to die; doctors want to save lives. We are back to the duality, to the idea that death is the opposite of life. And really you cannot go very far with that. You could come up with constructs of the after-life or reincarnation, but you are still just playing around with concepts; you are still trying to define death and life as being in the world when, as we have discussed, the world is just a screen. The world is just a projection. It is a screen into which meanings get read.

Although it runs against common experience, the body is not born, the body does not die, the body is not sick, and the body is not well. These are meanings that are read into the images of the world. The world is nothing more than dancing shadows that are given labels and meanings by the mind. We need to pull the discussion of death back to the larger context of the big picture, or down to a deeper level. Here are a couple of paragraphs from the Manual for Teachers that we can use as a springboard for our discussion:

> Death is the central dream from which all illusions stem. Is it not madness to think of life as being born, aging, losing vitality, and dying in the end? We have asked this question before, but now we need to consider it more carefully. It is the one fixed, unchangeable belief of the world that all things in it are born only to die. This is regarded as "the way of nature," not to be raised to question, but to be accepted as the "natural" law of life. The cyclical, the changing and unsure; the undependable and the unsteady, waxing and waning in a certain way upon a certain path – all this is taken as the Will of God and no one asks if a benign Creator could will this.
>
> In this perception of the universe as God created, it would be impossible to think of Him as loving. For who has decreed that all things pass away, ending in dust and disappointment and despair, can but be feared. He holds your little life in his hand but by a thread, ready to break it off without regret or care, perhaps today. Or if he waits, yet is the ending certain. Who loves such a god knows not of love, because he has denied that life is real. Death has become life's symbol. His world is now a battleground, where contradiction reigns and opposites make endless war. Where there is death is peace impossible. (M-27.1-2)

The beginning of the next page starts with:

> The "reality" of death is firmly rooted in the belief that God's Son is a body. And if God created bodies, death would indeed be real. But God would not be loving. (M-27.5)

We are back to our belief in the body, which is just a fragmentation of the belief that separation is possible. The belief in time and space makes distance possible, whether it is in a time sense or a spatial sense, and bodies and matter and the fragmentation just continue on and on and on. The perception is very twisted. Twisted perception is what death is. Death is to have an idea that God did not create held in mind and given reality. It is only by waking up – by looking at the ego and seeing its unreality – that death can be given up.

This can seem pretty abstract. Another way we can come at it is from more of an emotional approach. We can simplify it by narrowing it down to one question: *How do I feel?* The Course simplifies things by saying that you have but two emotions. One is love and one is fear. Love comes from choosing with the Holy Spirit and fear comes from choosing with the ego. Whenever the mind aligns with one or the other, the emotion that is produced is love or fear. Peace, contentedness, happiness and joy are all attributes or off-shoots of love. Hatred, anger, jealousy and depression are off-shoots of the emotion of fear. When one is feeling fear, or any of the derivatives of fear, then that is death. This is an indicator that the mind has chosen death. When one is peaceful, content, in a state of joy and feeling very connected, that is a state of love – an indicator that the mind has chosen the miracle, the mind has chosen life!

When we speak of Life, with a capital "L," we are again speaking of Knowledge or the Kingdom of Heaven which is purely abstract, infinite and eternal. It has nothing to do with time and space and bodies at all. In that sense, the miracle is like a reflection of Life. It is a decision; you can tell what decision you are making by the way that you feel.

Friend: So death is really not an ending or a change at all as we have usually thought of it in terms of death of the body?

David: In a sense, death is a change from the state of Life. It simplifies it by saying that there is just life and death. When one is upset, mildly annoyed, a tiny bit frustrated, angry, raging or depressed, the mind has chosen death. Regardless of the form of upset, it is a decision for death. It is like a hell on earth in the sense that the mind is in a state of fear.

Friend: So, just as health or sickness is a state of mind, death and life is a state of mind? None of it has anything to do with the body or the world or anything outside my mind?

David: That is why the Bible and the Course say that there is no death; what God Created is really all that exists. The hallucination of fear and pain or any form of upset is a miscreation or a fantasy, a fictitious made-up experience. To a mind that is asleep and dreaming it seems very real. It has been chosen. It is believed in, so it seems very real. We are not trying to dismiss those feelings because every one of us who has come to this planet has had those experiences. The Course is just telling us that there is something beyond these experiences and that they are not states of mind that come from God. God did not create fear.

Friend: Can you talk about the commonly held belief that when the body dies, the mind wakes up to Heaven or eternal peace? Of course, in the context of what you have just said, that makes no sense whatsoever.

## THE FINAL ILLUSION –
## THE BELIEF IN DEATH

David: In any instant Life is available as a choice. Even at the instant of the seeming death of the body, the mind can make a choice for Life.

Friend: So the death of the body does not automatically imply there is going to be eternal life?

David: Exactly. It is still an interpretation, a construct to attempt to explain things. It is believed that birth is real, that life in the world constitutes growing, aging and having experiences. It is believed that there is a linear life that one can look back on and even look forward to, and that the death of the body comes at the end of a span of life. Believing this the mind tries to make up something to reassure itself, like, *Even though this wasn't the most wonderful experience here on earth, God is waiting and as soon as I die I'll go to Heaven immediately.* Some believe that everyone goes to Heaven and some would say that everyone is judged and that some go to hell and some go to Heaven. There are all kinds of explanations, like reincarnation for example – keep evolving until you make it back to Source.

Ultimately those ideas are a justification for a mind that does not have a clue about what is happening. It would like to believe that is how the dilemma of conflict gets resolved. You simply die. The body dies and then the conflict is resolved. But try following that line of thinking; if it was something that had any resonance or truth to it, then why live in this world? Why continue on? Why not put the body to death as soon as possible, if Heaven waits? It is a kind of circular reasoning that does not make sense if really looked into. It is just an attempt to explain things. Mythologies throughout the ages in all cultures have attempted to explain the world and make some meaning out of it.

The metaphysics of the Course is about looking at the beliefs that made up the illusion of the world, without trying to find a source or a meaning *in* the world. Scientists look with their super long-range electronic telescopes for evidence of the Big Bang. They are still, from the perspective of scientific mythology so to speak, looking out in the world for the beginning. There is no beginning.

Friend: That is still looking at the inexplicable and trying to explain it.

David: Obviously there is a belief in the reality of it. That is why there is an attempt to explain it; it appears to be real. The world appears to be real because the five senses witness to the reality of it to a mind that wishes it to have a reality and a life of its own.

Friend: So the fear we heard expressed recently by our friend who was concerned that his body may die before he had the chance to really follow the path of ACIM and awaken, just doesn't hold water in this context because the awakening has no relationship to the life or death of the body as it is defined.

David: That is where fear comes in. There is a belief in the body. Of course, believing that the body is "me" or is where "I" exist, or is in some way associated with "who I am," then death of the body which seems to be an ending is a very fearful idea; it seems to be a termination of "me."

Even in the more sophisticated metaphysical systems that believe there is something that survives the death of the body–for instance a soul that goes on–when you take a close look at those ideas it still comes back to the question of what the source is of this thing that dies? Why does one part stay and another part split off and go on to something else? There is a sense of splitting, of duality. Even the deeper perspective of reincarnation is not metaphysically correct, though it can serve as a stepping stone to think that everyone continues to go through "lifetimes" or opportunities to learn lessons and that in the end, everyone returns to the Source.

That can be a comforting thought, but as you go deeper you come to see the falsity even of that. These lifetimes have a lot of aggravation and suffering and turmoil in them. What kind of God holds out the prize at the end of a long journey of lifetimes saying that you have to go through all this pain and suffering before you can come home? This still connects God with the perceptual world. You still have a God who in some way is connected to this world and is in some way connected to the pain and suffering. If He even *knows* about the perceptual world and is deciding to stay aloof until this and that happens, we get back to this idea of an all-powerful, all-knowing, all-loving God who is not tinkering and tampering with the suffering of his children.

Friend: Not very loving then.

David: No. Where did the *all-loving* attribute go?

Friend: Or he is all-loving but does not really have the power to do that—it is out of His control.

David: Omnipotence kind of disappears as a quality at that point. With the Course we have a metaphor of the Holy Spirit who sees the illusions in the mind but knows they are not real. But even the Holy Spirit is metaphorically God's representative or the remembrance of God. God knows not form and in that sense God knows not about suffering. God knows what He Created and *only* what He Created and that is Spirit. That is Love.

Let's read a couple of sentences from Chapter 27 in the Manual for Teachers that are very helpful. We'll start with the second-to-last paragraph:

> And the last to be overcome will be death. Of course! Without the idea of death there is no world. All dreams will end with this one. This is salvation's final goal; the end of all illusions. (M-27.6)

And from the bottom of the last paragraph:

> And what is the end of death? Nothing but this; the realization that the Son of God is guiltless now and forever. Nothing but this. But do not let yourself forget it is not less than this. (M-27.7)

## THE MEANING OF THE RESURRECTION

Friend: Now we are back to the resurrection, which is the next topic in the Manual for Teachers. Let's start by addressing the resurrection of Jesus, which is what usually comes to mind when speaking of resurrection.

David: We began our discussion of death by saying that the common usage of the word death involved death of the body. In the same sense the resurrection of Jesus seems to involve a body as does the also famous resurrection of Lazarus, which was about a body coming back to life. We have just gone through the fact that the body is not born, does not die, does not get sick, and does not get well, etc., though all appearances are to the contrary. To the mind that believes in this, these things all seem possible; it seems that they happen. The belief in appearances makes them seem to be more than just a screen. The resurrection of Jesus was a tremendous teaching example taken in the context of his life and his teachings, such as, "Jesus answered and said unto them, destroy this temple, and in three days I will raise it up." (John 2:19) He told his apostles and some of his followers exactly what would happen and went through the crucifixion, defenseless, completely demonstrating everything that he taught in his life.

Friend: So Jesus had no belief in the death of the body?

David: No. He *knew* that he was Spirit. He was at the mind level and he knew he was Spirit and that death of the body was literally nothing; he knew that it was completely insignificant. Basically our story of crucifixion and resurrection is a great teaching example of the insignificance of the body and the power of the mind; a mind that is well-aligned with the Father knows Life and is the manifestation of Life.

Friend: And the example that Jesus left through his bodily death and the resurrection really has the power it does because he did not have any belief in death of the body.

David: It was just a demonstration to the world. Obviously the world and the deceived mind believe very strongly in the world as being life. Birth is described as the regeneration of life; it is not seen as just a projection. There is no life in the world or of the world. It is only the mind which is choosing with the Holy Spirit – the mind that is lined up with the Right Mind – that experiences Life. We can shift it back to the mind level again as we did with the idea of death. The Manual for Teachers states this as follows:

> Very simply, the resurrection is the overcoming or surmounting of death. It is a reawakening or a rebirth; a

change of mind about the meaning of the world. It is
the acceptance of the Holy Spirit's interpretation of the
world's purpose; the acceptance of the Atonement for
oneself. It is the end of dreams of misery, and the glad
awareness of the Holy Spirit's final dream. It is the recognition of the gifts of God. It is the dream in which
the body functions perfectly, having no function except
communication. It is the lesson in which learning ends,
for it is consummated and surpassed with this. It is the
invitation to God to take His final step. (M-28.1)

And probably most importantly:

It is the relinquishment of all other purposes, all other
interests, all other wishes and all other concerns. It is the
single desire of the Son for the Father. (M-28.1)

The reason I say "most importantly" is that this is the giving up
of the belief in the world. All the goals and aims that the mind
attempts to pursue in the world are literally that which keeps
Life blocked from awareness in the mind. They go hand in hand.
You cannot simultaneously fulfill your one function here and
have other functions. Those other functions must be laid aside to
live out your one function as an expression of God. It all comes
back to changing the mind about the meaning of the world. The
world was made as an attack on God and the ego uses the screen,
the world it sees, to keep the mind distracted from looking at
these beliefs in the mind.

To have a new meaning for the world is to question all of the purposes, meanings and goals that one has had for it, including the
uses of the body. Ask the Holy Spirit to help sort out in the mind
the true from the false, and then lay aside the false. The resurrection is a decision, a final letting go of all strivings, purposes and
desires, leaving only the desire for the Father.

Friend: So the resurrection of Jesus preceded what we think of as his physical resurrection, is that right?

David: If you are thinking of it as in time, then yes. He says that the resurrection is the acceptance of the Atonement for oneself. This is a decision that is made in the mind and, as we have just read, the body functions perfectly after that decision. In other words, once the decision is made, the body is simply a vehicle to be used by the Holy Spirit to let the light shine into the world so to speak, to let the Spirit be demonstrated to the world. In that sense, the Atonement is a decision and it appears to be a decision Jesus made before the crucifixion. The drama of the crucifixion and the resurrection were all part of the teaching example that was to be left for the world to see.

Of course when we talk about *when* Jesus accepted the Atonement, we are still speaking in metaphors. As the Course says, the Atonement is a decision that the teacher of God must make and there is only one time that the Atonement can be accepted. That time is *now*. The ego can go on and on with fascinating and ingenious questions about things such as when in his life Jesus accepted the Atonement, but on a subtle level these are distractions away from the central point that Jesus makes – that the teacher of God, the student of the Course, has to accept that decision for the Atonement for himself. This is the sole responsibility of the miracle worker.

## MIND TRAINING AND THE ACIM WORKBOOK

David: The next question is usually, "OK, having heard that, how do I do it?" This is a very common question. The answer is that we have in the Course a tool for awakening, a curriculum to follow. We have a Text, a Workbook and a Manual for Teachers. These are to be *applied*, not just read or talked about. When he gives instructions in the Workbook to do certain things, to try to remember a specific thought so many times a day or to apply a thought to particular things in the room – this is a training program for the mind! It is a very practical training program that has been given to the deceived mind to be used to wake up – to make that final decision for the Atonement. Resistance is experienced because the mind is still split between the ego and the Holy Spirit. As anyone who has attempted to work with the Course knows, the ego is very, very resistant to learning this curriculum, because it is literally the undoing of the ego.

Friend: That's where the mind-watching comes in that you talk about. Do you want to go into that a little bit?

David: There are a number of passages in the Workbook designed to train the mind to step back from thoughts and watch them, as dispassionately as possible. For example, lesson 10 says to search your mind for thoughts, without judging or classifying them in anyway; "…you might imagine that you are watching an oddly assorted procession going by, which has little if any personal meaning to you." (W-10.4)

At one point Jesus says, "You are much too tolerant of mind wandering." (T-2.VI.4) You must always keep watch of your mind; "be vigilant only for God and His Kingdom." (T-6.V.C) The mind has to be trained to be attentive to the thoughts. Once again, it is about the two thought systems in the mind. The Holy Spirit's thought system is referred to as your "real thoughts;" the ego's fear-based thought system is referred to as your "unreal thoughts," or "attack thoughts." The mind has to sort out and discern between these two thought systems. Once the fear-based thought system is relinquished, all that is left are the real thoughts. The light in the mind has been covered over by cloudbanks of attack thoughts.

Friend: So the untrained mind is basically just full of unreal thoughts? The mind is blank, as one of the lessons says.

David: When the mind is invested in these attack thoughts – that did *not* come from God – then the mind thinks that it is thinking real thoughts. It thinks it is in a real world because these thoughts are projected and show up, so to speak, on the screen as a world. There seems to be an inner world and an outer world. For example, one can say, "Boy, I'm sure glad I didn't say what I was thinking there," as if what they are saying in the world is one thing and what they are thinking is another. The Workbook is a means of training the mind to see that the thoughts you think you think are not real. Ultimately even though you think you are thinking, your mind is literally blank when it is preoccupied with attack thoughts, which include all thoughts of the past and of the future.

Friend: So any thinking that has a component of form is not thinking at all, is that right?

David: I think it might be more helpful to use the distinction of time, to say that any thought constructed about the past or the future is not thinking. The real thoughts I think and feel are a metaphor for the miracle or true perception. True perception still involves form; it is still perceptual. But all meaning of a past tense and a future tense has been removed from it. It is like a blank slate with no meaning read into the form except for the Holy Spirit's one purpose, which then frees the mind. That is the real world.

Attack thoughts represent distorted perception. Once these thoughts have been questioned, and once the mind has been able to dis-identify or dispassionately watch these thoughts and see them as merely false without investing in them and believing in them, then we get down to the real thoughts which are representative of the real world or the healed mind.

Friend: And do the unreal thoughts diminish as that occurs?

David: The word "diminish" still makes it quantifiable. I think the best way of coming at it is what Jesus says, "…the ego fades away and is undone." (T-5.IV.1) The thoughts fade; they become more distant, more peripheral and less noticed as attention is withdrawn from them. They just fade and fade and fade.

Friend: So the attention of the mind is given to the real thoughts instead?

## MIND-WATCHING AND
## THE DECISION FOR PEACE

David: Yes, which is automatic once the mind stays focused on the Atonement; the mind is protected by the Atonement. One cannot have attention on the Atonement and on those thoughts as well. It is one of those either/or decisions. So when the mind becomes very good at consistently choosing the miracle and keeping its attention on the Atonement, then the attack thoughts begin to fade because attention and investment has been withdrawn from them.

In the ultimate sense, we can speak of Thought, with a capital T, as being Christ. In other words, Jesus describes Christ as a Thought or an Idea in the Mind of God. You notice how that is a capital T and it is singular. Singular is very important here because even real thoughts still have a plural sense; there is still a bit of perception involved even though the wheat and the chaff have been separated out so to speak. The Thought of God,

Christ, is literally beyond perception. Christ and the Father are part of the Kingdom of Heaven and part of the state of Knowledge, with a capital K, which again just *is*. It does not involve form in any way.

Friend: So can we go back to the mind-watching in terms of how to do that, the practical application? Just bring it down into the everyday a little bit more if you can.

David: The early lessons work at helping the mind to see that there really is no difference between the inner and the outer. This is a very fundamental principle in the undoing of the false. The first lesson starts out, "Nothing I see means anything." "Nothing I *see*." Right away we are talking about perception and objects that seem to be in the room. This is followed by a lesson, "I have given everything I see all the meaning it has for me." This brings perception back to the mind: "*I* have given…" The mind is reading meaning into everything it sees. The ideas presented in the Workbook go back and forth between the "inner" and "outer." They focus on thinking versus perceiving. Lesson number 5, "I am never upset for the reason I *think*." Here we are talking about upset but we are also talking about *thoughts*, "I am never upset for the reason I think." Followed by lesson 6, "I am upset because I *see* something that is not there." Here comes perception back in to the picture. If you look closely at the early lessons you will see that he goes back and forth between *thinking* and the *mind*, and *perceiving* which is seen to be something separate from thinking, something different from my private world of thoughts.

The early lessons are the initial attempt to help with the mind-watching, and of course the Text is so important because it gives the whole theoretical basis for sorting out these two thought systems that the deceived mind is completely confused about.

There is a section in the Course (T-14.X.5) about a weaving, changing pattern of darkness and light that continuously sweeps across the horizon of the mind. This is a powerful mind that has accepted darkness, has accepted the falsity of attack thoughts, so there are sweeping patterns of darkness and light. This is analogous to the noise and chatter that one hears in the mind. It is not just the pure, still tranquility of light. There are these alternating patterns.

Mind-watching is something one can do not only when stilling the mind in the more traditional sense of meditation; you can do it while moving through the activities of the day, while watching a movie or having a conversation; you can notice your thoughts even when you are reading a book. It is not really something you are doing; "doing" isn't quite the right word—but you can be aware of your thoughts.

Friend: So is it noticing the thoughts—noticing whether a thought is of God or of the ego?

David: That comes more in the advanced stages of mind-watching, when there starts to be some clarity and real discernment. Then it becomes more and more obvious.

Friend: But initially, it's just simply noticing what the thoughts are, because the untrained mind has thoughts that it is not even aware of? The whole point is to become aware, first of all, of the thoughts that are there and then at some point to begin discerning which thought system each of those thoughts relates to?

David: Yes. It takes quite a lot of training just to be able to start to watch one's emotions and thoughts because it means going back into the mind, working at the metaphysical level. The world was made as a distractive device to keep the attention *away* from the mind, so there is a strong emphasis on form and on differences. It can take many forms. For instance, using television to just numb out and focus on the screen, like a fantasy world or a day dream. The images on the screen are so absorbing that one does not have to think about anything. Mind-watching on the other hand is a process of looking at thoughts and noticing feelings.

Friend: And not just during meditation, but continuously. That is really what you are suggesting and what the Course suggests, to make it an ongoing, moment-by-moment sort of thing.

David: You are speaking of more an advanced stage. In the beginning – if you look at the early lessons – there is a minute here and a minute there. Jesus knows how untrained the deceived mind is and therefore begins with very small incremental steps with no attempt at an elaborate discipline or structure. It builds as the lessons go on. The lessons are designed to be used by someone who does not have a lot of time to be quiet or to pull back in meditation. In the beginning one can just carry an idea forth into the day, applying the idea during specific time frames. As one progresses through the Workbook this gets transferred and applied more and more consistently. One becomes more voluntarily vigilant once the value of the mind-watching is recognized.

Friend: So the thought of the day that the Workbook lesson gives is an anchor or a thought of God that can be in the mind? I'm sure that Jesus knows that most of the time it is not the thought of God that is in the untrained mind, so the intent would be to have it available in contrast to what is usually there? I guess it is really by contrast that the mind realizes that the thought of God is mostly not in the mind. Most of the time there is something other than that there.

David: In other traditions it can go by the name of "mantra" or "affirmations." At the beginning the mind is *so* untrained that a central idea to keep the attention on is a way of keeping it focused and in a sense, a way of controlling thoughts. This is not always so easy at first. Even with the thought for the day, one will notice the mind wanting to wander away. Restlessness or forgetting the thought is quite a common experience. This is just an indicator of how untrained the mind is. It is not something to feel guilty about. If you try to judge how well you are doing or start comparing, the guilt will enter in. Mind-watching requires willingness and gentleness, and a lot of persistence.

Friend: Dedication is what comes to my mind. You said that a lot of effort is required to do this initially but after doing it over and over again and seeing the value and benefit of it, it seems to require less effort. So can you talk about the benefit, the value that you have found for yourself in the mind-watching such that it has actually become an attractive force?

## THE GOAL OF A COURSE IN MIRACLES

David: The stated goal of *A Course in Miracles* is peace of mind. You start to get glimpses of this peace. In the beginning it may be fleeting glimpses. There can be a lot of stuff that comes up that really needs to be looked at; that can be experienced as painful. But with consistency and persistence you begin to move forward, to put one foot in front of the other. With practice it gets easier to generalize principles to a wider and wider range of situations, people, and circumstances. There comes a greater consistency of thought. This is the advanced mind-training. The peace that is experienced is wonderful. It is wonderful to be at peace and to *not* choose to be upset so to speak. Once the thoughts and the beliefs have been looked at and questioned, there starts to be discernment in the mind between the true and the false, the real and the unreal. There is a pulling back from the investment in the thoughts as they are watched dispassionately. Peace becomes more stable.

There are still points where twinges and reactions come up, but more and more there is a strong emotional experience or awareness that my state is a result of my decision, *not* the result of what is happening on the screen, such as the way people seem to be treating me. It is not a result of conditions such as the economy, weather, or finances, or any of the endless list of false causes the deceived mind comes up with. These external things are recognized more and more as projections.

Mind-watching, going within, and questioning beliefs about everything perceived in this world, leads to peace. The belief in being an individual person, a body with unique attributes and likes and dislikes all has to be questioned and voluntarily stepped back from or dis-identified from. Then the peace becomes stable and the joy very intense! It is like finding the pearl of great value that Jesus talks about in the Bible and immediately selling everything because there is just such great joy! This is the key mankind has been looking for, the key to peace of mind, to the Kingdom of Heaven. The Course per se is not the only key; it is just one tool among many. But it certainly is a very helpful tool for dis-identifying from unreal thoughts and learning to maintain a consistent state of mind.

Friend: The peace of mind is the key. *A Course in Miracles* is a helpful tool for finding that key; the door is always there to open it with.

David: It is about having one goal as opposed to having many, many, many goals. Peace of mind is an abstract goal, an experiential goal, as opposed to completing a project, achieving a certain status, finding the right partner or making a particular amount of money. Those external goals just begin to fade and fall to the wayside because the one goal of peace is held out in all situations and conditions. This is seemingly very unnatural for the deceived mind. The deceived mind is conditioned to focus on concrete, specific goals and expectations. This is why the mind training takes time.

You have to begin to recognize that form-goals have not brought peace of mind and that by holding on to this abstract goal of peace, a complete change can take place in your state of mind. To go to a board room meeting for example, and have only peace as your goal might seem a bit ludicrous if you are thinking in terms of a purpose such as presenting or discussing specific corporate objectives. The moment any of these form-based goals rise up as a priority over peace, they will literally block the way; conflict and disagreements will follow automatically because there is a perceived separate interest. You cannot have a perceived separate interest unless you perceive yourself as a separate person, a self that is separate from your brother. The idea of personhood has to be identified before any of this can enter in.

Friend: I have a question. How can I continue to function within anything that holds objectives and goals that are form goals, whether it is a work setting, an organization of which I'm a member, a family, a marriage, or a country? How can I function within a context that has form goals if I am determined to have only the one goal of peace?

# THE INNER AND OUTER ARE ONE

David: We have to take a look at the assumptions in your question. Remember, the inner and the outer are not different. Your question is *How can "I" function? How can "I," a person, function in a context that has other goals?* You are implying that the institution in which you are working has goals. Institutions do not have goals. Institutions are ideas in the mind that are projected outward. Situations and families do not have goals in and of themselves. There is no objective society that is outside of the mind. There are no objective institutions or workplaces or families that have different goals than the self. There is only the mind that holds onto concepts and the mind can hold conflicting goals. So the belief in personhood, that subject/object split that we have talked about – the inner and the outer being the same instead of different – is a very central point in answering your question.

Friend: You are saying the question really stands on making that distinction between the inner and the outer. So the question is really a statement?

David: Yes. The question stands on the assumption that there *is* an inner and an outer. For instance, the idea that this workplace has goals that seem to be different than my goal for peace; there is a conflict here. It is not seen that the institution itself is a concept in the mind.

There is nothing outside of you; the world is simply a world of ideas in the mind, projected out. Once projected, the mind forgets that it is simply one's own projection or dream. The world is perceived through the body's senses. The mind thinks that it is a person in a world that is objectively different from it. It is believed that the person is the subject, having a subjective experience, and the world is the object – whether it is the world of family, business, community, nation, planet, or cosmos. That world is seen to be objectively different than the "me," the small "me." Your question presumes that. Now, this is very deep and abstract; it is very ultimate in that it actually contains the release. If you can begin to grasp this then you have your foot in the door to being released from all conflict.

The Holy Spirit has to work with that mind to help it see that these constructs are nothing more than concepts. They do not have any reality. The Holy Spirit works with the mind where it believes it is. For instance, in working with the Course the first lesson does not ask you to lay aside all thoughts, concepts and beliefs that you have ever held about the world. No. The Workbook starts off with the lesson, "Nothing I see means anything." It is a simple lesson in beginning to detach from the meaning of things that the physical eyes see. It is a first glimmer of the idea that seeing is *not* believing. There is a spark of the idea that there is something beyond what I see with the naked eye, so to speak.

## SEEING THINGS DIFFERENTLY

David: The Workbook lessons can be applied by taking the idea for the day into a work, church, or laundromat setting, or wherever one seems to go. The idea helps to loosen the mind's grip on the concepts. There is a gradual loosening of concepts. Detachment seems to come step by step, little by little. When you hold peace as your goal, you will begin to detach from the ways of the world, in the mind. There may be form changes in the seeming lifestyle on the screen as well, but these will just be reflections of changes in the mind.

Friend: It seems like there would almost have to be form changes that would just automatically follow from the changes in the mind. As the mind loosens up the form would loosen up.

David: When you study the lives of saints, this is what you see. When we say study the *life*, we may look at what the body seemed to be doing in form, but when we talk about life we are really talking about the mind. When you study the teachings of wonderful teachers such as Ramana Maharshi, Meher Baba, Krishnamurti, and of course Jesus, you hear them speak of detachment. You see it demonstrated in their lives and in the lives of all mystics. The Buddha talked about how all grief comes from attachment. This idea has been around for a long time. We do not see these beings struggling with bosses or family members; they clearly see that the mind is the cause of the dream world and that one is never the helpless victim of circumstances and events in the world.

I am not in the world; the world is in my mind. I can choose to detach from the ego's purpose, which is to use the world to reinforce the conflict in the mind and to maintain the belief in separation, or I can detach and forgive and overlook the appearances of the world. I am the dreamer of the dream; I can choose to give the thoughts, the world, and my mind another purpose. I do not have to answer to the dream figures because I hear only one Voice. I hear the Voice for God.

Friend: The wisdom is really the recognition of who I am?

David: There is great power in that recognition. Defenselessness and strength go together. Innocence and strength are attributes, in the metaphysical perspective, that go together. This is not so in the world. One who is defenseless is seen to be a pushover, vulnerable to being mowed down and victimized by this mighty external world. But the saint or the mystic sees that the world is not external. I am not a little body in this giant, external world. As a matter of fact, this body and the other bodies and the world itself are simply projections. There is no fear of projections in a healed mind.

I assure you that as you continue to take one step in front of the other, following the voice within and applying the principles, this will all seem very natural. You will not need to rely on the kind of people pleasing and co-dependencies that a mind unsure of its own identity needs to prop itself up. All true self-esteem and self-worth come from remembering one's true Identity as Spirit and dis-identifying from all the projections in the external world. It is about seeing the blocks for what they are and simply withdrawing belief and investment from them. It really is that simple.

## THE BELIEF IN SACRIFICE

Friend: I would like to go into the whole concept of sacrifice. I believe the idea of sacrifice is kind of a misconception. Can you say something about it?

David: Well, to a deceived mind that believes in the world, the world is obviously *something*. It is something "important." It has existence and it has importance. If we get back to the idea of ordering thoughts and our discussion about the hierarchy of illusions, we see there are some elements of the perceived world that have been given more importance than others. Letting go of any projection that has value to the mind would be perceived as a sacrifice. It is only the awareness of the *lack of value* of the projection that completely eliminates the idea of sacrifice. Sacrifice comes from placing value in idols.

Friend: And then feeling like something has to be forfeited for some reason? I guess it is always for the purpose of getting something that is considered more valuable, something that you are willing to sacrifice for?

David: The idol is seen as having more value than this hypothetical thing called salvation or peace. Peace is perceived as a nice idea, a utopian idea. It is seen as having blind faith in something unseen, like God, or the Holy Spirit. The mind is still afraid of this light. It is still uncertain about the Spirit. The form, the concrete, has become familiar and comfortable. It believes in clinging to the old, familiar and comfortable rather than to that which it sees as a risk, rather than opening up to something that it is unsure of.

Obviously, hand in hand with laying aside beliefs in the world comes the development of trust. One has to develop trust in the Holy Spirit, to develop trust in the unseen as being actually the "reality" of things, and to follow that, to lay aside investment in the world. Without the development of trust, the belief in sacrifice clicks in because it is a very deep cornerstone of the ego's thought system. The belief that it is a sacrifice to give up the things runs very, very deep.

Friend: So the mind really has to have some confidence that there is something else it is going toward before it is ready to let go of what it knows?

David: Sacrifice "…always means the giving up of what you want. And what, O teacher of God, is it that you want?" (M-13.6) In other words, "Is it a sacrifice to give up pain?" (M-13.4)

## PLEASURE AND PAIN – IS IT A SACRIFICE TO GIVE THEM UP?

David: Is it a sacrifice to give up pain? Pain is the belief in this world, the belief in the body, the belief in the twisted perception that is literally death. The investment in death is *painful.* It is painful to maintain belief in something that is not true. Those who seek for answers in this world are seeking for happiness and salvation where it cannot be found. And this is painful. The giving up of judgment, the giving up of the ordering of thoughts and so on, is literally *the giving up of pain!* Is it a sacrifice to give up pain?

Friend: Only to a mind that doesn't recognize that this *is* pain.

David: Yes, exactly.

Friend: And the undoing is to recognize just what you said, that there is nothing here.

David: As we said earlier, pleasure and pain are two sides of the same coin. You cannot seek for pleasure without finding pain. It is a disguise; the body's pleasure, to the ego, is good. It whispers to the mind that this is good. To itself it whispers, *This is death.* The ego does not want the mind to see the trick of pursuing pleasure.

To the deceived mind pleasure is one of the greatest things in the dream world. If this is a kingdom apart from the abstract Spirit of God, pleasure is perceived as being one of the best things going. The deceived mind believes it is a cruel, wicked, dog-eat-dog world. *All this pain, sickness and suffering but at least, thank heavens, we have pleasure!* Pleasure is seen as a release, a respite from misery, loneliness and despair. What the ego does not let on is that the investment in pleasure, which is obviously of the body, reinforces the body as being real in the mind's awareness. "You see the flesh or recognize the spirit." (T-31.VI.1) Jesus is clearly saying that it is one or the other; you cannot have both. In the ultimate sense there is no reconciliation between Spirit and the time-space-matter continuum. The closest you come to the leaping-off point is true perception or a happy dream, which is still a leaping-off point. Knowledge and the happy dream do not have a meeting point. The mind has to be trained to come to true perception, to come to the real world or the happy dream, so that God can take the final step. This training is the step that God or the Holy Spirit requires, metaphorically speaking.

The Holy Spirit overlooks pleasure as He overlooks pain. People easily accept that the Holy Spirit overlooks the painful aspects of the world, but there are passages in the Course where we see pleasure just as readily overlooked. "A tiny stab of pain, a little worldly pleasure…" is one way it is stated. (T-27.VI.6) The Holy Spirit simply does not look to *effects*; the world of sensations, pleasurable or painful and everything in between are not in the domain of the Spirit. The Holy Spirit does not see the body as the deceived mind sees it at all. It always comes back to giving up the values of the world. And as we said, the mind will perceive it as sacrifice to give up the values of the world unless you can see that they are painful, regardless of how they seem to be experienced. Once you see that pleasure and pain are two sides of the same coin you will come to the recognition that this is true.

In any single instant the attraction of guilt would be experienced as painful but within the projected world of time and space it gets spread out over time so that the mind can believe it is a person that has both painful and pleasurable experiences. "At no single instant does the body exist at all. It is always remembered or anticipated, but never experienced just now." (T-18.VII.3) We can look back and ruminate about how painful or pleasurable experiences were – but they are *all* mis-creations, mis-thoughts. The mind is *blank*. The mind is not thinking at all. The mind is covering over the holy instant.

Friend: That's taking it in deeply.

David: We are getting down to the core of things now. We are not dancing around the periphery anymore. We are down to the core, to the basics of it. And there is joy! There is immense release, immense joy that comes when the mind gets clear on this, when the mind no longer buys into the tricks of the ego, when it listens to the Holy Spirit! The Holy Spirit's lessons are joyful. When the mind is learning what it perceives as painful lessons it is because there is a decision being made for the ego. One does not choose the Holy Spirit as the Advisor and experience pain. Joy, peace, love and the feeling of connectedness with the Spirit is experienced *in contrast* to the pain. It is the contrast between the two that impels the mind to move toward the joy by choosing with the Holy Spirit.

## THE HOLY SPIRIT AND THE CALL TO JOY

David: We have to have something to rely on daily, as all our distorted beliefs are surfacing in awareness. As we are working through the lessons of forgiveness and looking at the false self-concepts, we need something we can feel close to. The Course calls that something the Holy Spirit. It goes by many names in various traditions – the inner voice, intuition, the small still voice…. Here is a helpful collection of quotes from the Course about the Holy Spirit:

> The Holy Spirit is the Spirit of joy. He is the Call to return with which God blessed the minds of His separated Sons. (T-5.II.2)

> The Holy Spirit is the Call to awaken and be glad. (T-5. II.10)

> How can you wake children in a more kindly way than by a gentle Voice that will not frighten them, but will merely remind them that the night is over and the light has come? (T-6.V.2)

115

The Holy Spirit sees the world as a teaching device for bringing you Home. (T-5.III.11)

The Holy Spirit's teaching takes only one direction and has only one goal. His direction is freedom and His goal is God. (T-8.II.6)

Any direction that will lead you where the Holy Spirit leads you not, goes nowhere. (T-8.II.6)

The opposite of joy is depression. When your learning promotes depression instead of joy, you cannot be listening to God's joyous Teacher and learning His lessons. (T-8.VII.13)

The Holy Spirit is your Guide in choosing. He is in the part of your mind that always speaks for the right choice, because He speaks for God. (T-5.II.8)

The Holy Spirit's Voice is as loud as your willingness to listen. It cannot be louder without violating your freedom of choice, which the Holy Spirit seeks to restore, never to undermine. (T-8.VIII.8)

The Holy Spirit will direct you only so as to avoid pain. Surely no one would object to this goal if he recognized it. The problem is not whether what the Holy Spirit says is true, but whether you want to listen to what He says. (T-7.X.3)

The Voice of the Holy Spirit does not command, because It is incapable of arrogance. It does not demand, because It does not seek control. It does not overcome, because It does not attack. It merely reminds. (T-5.II.7)

It is only because you think that you can run some little part, or deal with certain aspects of your life alone, that the guidance of the Holy Spirit is limited. (T-14.XI.8)

Do you really believe you can plan for your safety and joy better than He can? You need be neither careful nor careless; you need merely cast your cares upon Him because He careth for you. (T-5.VII.1)

Be comforted, and feel the Holy Spirit watching over you in love and perfect confidence in what He sees. (T-20.V.8)

Complexity is not of God. How could it be when all He knows is One? He knows of One creation, One Reality, One Truth and but One Son. Nothing conflicts with Oneness. How, then, could there be complexity in Him? What is there to decide? For it is conflict that makes choice possible. The truth is simple; it is one, without an opposite. And how could strife enter in its simple presence, and bring complexity where oneness is? The truth makes no decisions, for there is nothing to decide *between*. And only if there were could choosing be a necessary step in the advance toward oneness. What is everything leaves room for nothing else. Yet is this magnitude beyond the scope of this curriculum. Nor is it necessary we dwell on anything that cannot be immediately grasped. (T-26.III.1)

This is a definitive statement that goes beyond all metaphors. It hints of a state that is beyond metaphor, a state of Knowledge. *A Course in Miracles* basically deals with decisions in the realm of the dream, training the mind to make a decision for the Holy Spirit—for the right mind. In the split mind it seems there is a choice; train the mind to look closely and distinguish between the seeming alternatives for choice. Although it is metaphorical, the mind that believes that it has separated from its Creator must make choices. *A Course in Miracles* is simply a course in making a better choice where a mistaken choice was made before.

## THE BORDERLAND OF THOUGHT

David: Let's read now from a section called *The Borderland*:

> There is a borderland of thought that stands between this world and Heaven. It is not a place and when you reach it is apart from time. Here is the meeting place where thoughts are brought together; where conflicting values meet and all illusions are laid down beside the truth, where they are judged to be untrue. This borderland is just beyond the gate of Heaven. Here is every thought made pure and wholly simple. Here is sin denied, and everything that *is*, received instead. This is the journey's end. We have referred to it as the real world. (T-26.III.2)

This is another description of the right mind, of the state of mind that is available when one consistently chooses the Holy Spirit, consistently chooses the right mind and lays aside the desire for the wrong mind.

## THE LITTLE HINDRANCE

David: If we move several sections ahead to *The Little Hindrance*, we can start to get a grasp of the Course's outline of time and the meaning of time. We will begin with the second paragraph:

> Nothing is ever lost but time, which in the end, is meaningless. For it is but a little hindrance to eternity, quite meaningless to the real Teacher of the world. Yet, since you do believe in it, why should you waste it going nowhere when it can be used to reach a goal as high as learning can achieve? Think not the way to Heaven's gate is difficult at all. Nothing you undertake with certain purpose and high resolve and happy confidence, holding your brothers hand and keeping step to Heaven's song, is difficult to do. But it is hard indeed to wander off, alone and miserable down a road that leads to nothing and that has no purpose.
>
> God gave His Teacher to replace the one you made, not to conflict with it. And what He would replace has been replaced. Time lasted but an instant in your mind with no effect upon eternity. And so is all time past, and everything exactly as it was before the way to nothingness was made. The tiny tick of time in which the first mistake was made, and all of them within that one mistake, held also the Correction for that one, and all of them that came within the first. And in that tiny instant time was gone, for that was all it ever was. What God gave answer to is answered and is gone.
>
> To you who still believe you live in time and know not it is gone, the Holy Spirit still guides you through the infinitely small and senseless maze you still perceive in time, though it has long since gone. You think you live

in what is past. Each thing you look upon you saw but for an instant, long ago, before its unreality gave way to truth. Not one illusion still remains unanswered in your mind. Uncertainty was brought to certainty so long ago that it is hard indeed to hold it to your heart, as if it were before you still.

The tiny instant you would keep and make eternal, passed away in Heaven too soon for anything to notice it had come. What disappeared too quickly to affect the simple knowledge of the Son of God can hardly still be there, for you to choose to be your teacher. Only in the past – an ancient past, too short to make a world in answer to creation – did this world appear to rise. So very long ago, for such a tiny interval of time, that not one note in Heaven's song was missed. Yet, in each unforgiving act or thought, in every judgment and in all belief in sin, is that one instant still called back, as if it could be made again in time. You keep an ancient memory before your eyes. And he who lives in memories alone is unaware of where he is. (T-26.V.2-5)

This is saying that the perceptual world of time and space was over and done a long time ago and that images, although they are still being called forth, are all past. It is quite a statement. If we move over to the next page, we find the statement:

Now you are shifting back and forth between the past and present. Sometimes the past seems real, as if it *were* the present. Voices from the past are heard and then are doubted. You are like to one who still hallucinates, but lacks conviction in what he perceives. This is the borderland between the worlds, the bridge between the past and present. Here the shadow of the past remains, but still a present light is dimly recognized. Once it is seen, this light can never be forgotten. It must draw you from the past into the present, where you really are.

The shadow voices do not change the laws of time nor of eternity. They come from what is past and gone, and hinder not the true existence of the here and now. The real world is the second part of the hallucination time and death are real, and have existence that can be perceived. This terrible illusion was denied in but the time it took for God to give His Answer to illusion for all time and every circumstance. And then it was no more to be experienced as there.

Each day, and every minute in each day, and every instant in that each minute holds, you but relive the single instant when the time of terror took the place of love. And so you die each day to live again, until you cross the gap between the past and present, which is not a gap at all. Such is each life; a seeming interval from birth to death and on to life again, a repetition of an instant gone by long ago that cannot be relived. And all of time is but the mad belief that what is over is still here and now. Forgive the past and let it go, for it *is* gone. (T-26.V.11-14)

This is a great commentary on the deepest levels of the self-concept. The ego's perception of time is linear; time goes forward and the past repeats itself in the future, skipping over the present. The Course tells us that the present and the past do not have a meeting place. Every present instant is a newborn chance for the mind to be free of the past completely.

# THE IMMEDIACY OF SALVATION

Now we move ahead to the section *The Immediacy of Salvation*:

The one remaining problem that you have is that you see an interval between the time when you forgive, and will receive the benefits of trusting in your brother. This but reflects the little you would keep between yourselves, that you might be a little separate. For time and space are one illusion, which takes different forms. If it has been projected beyond your mind you think of it as time. The nearer it is brought to where it is, the more you think of it in terms of space.

There is a distance you would keep apart from one another, and this space you see as time because you still believe you are external to your brother. This makes trust impossible. And you cannot believe that trust would settle every problem now. Thus do you think it safer to remain a little careful and a little watchful of interests perceived as separate. From this perception you cannot conceive of gaining what forgiveness offers *now*. The interval you think lies in between the giving and the receiving of the gift seems to be one in which you sacrifice and suffer loss. You see eventual salvation, not immediate results.

Salvation *is* immediate. Unless you so perceive it, you will be afraid of it, believing that the risk of loss is great between the time its purpose is made yours and its effects will come to you. In this form is the error still obscured that is the source of fear. Salvation *would* wipe out the space you see between you still, and let you instantly become as one. And it is here you fear the loss would lie. Do not project this fear to time, for time is not the enemy that you perceive. Time is as neutral as the body is, except in terms of what you see it for. If you would keep a little space between you still, you want a little time in which forgiveness is withheld a little while. This makes the interval between the time in which forgiveness is withheld and given seem dangerous, with terror justified.

Yet space between you is apparent *now*, and cannot be perceived in future time. No more can it be overlooked except within the present. Future loss is not your fear. But present joining is your dread. Who can feel desolation except now? A future cause as yet has no effects. And therefore must it be that if you fear, there is a present cause. And it is *this* that needs correction, not a future state. (T-26.VIII.1-4)

David: This is the metaphysical distinction that *A Course in Miracles* makes: all of the pain, the guilt, the discomfort and the fear that are ever experienced are not because of something that is happening out in the world or something that has happened long ago. It is all due to a present decision in the mind to hold onto a past cause or to hold onto a belief that has no existence in reality, a belief that is truly over, done and gone.

To continue:

The plans you make for safety are all laid within the future, where you cannot plan. No purpose has been given it as yet, and what will happen has as yet no cause. Who can predict effects without a cause? And who could fear effects unless he thought they had been caused, and judged disastrous *now*? Belief in sin arouses fear, and like its cause, is looking forward, looking back, but overlooking what is here and now. Yet only here and now its cause must be, if its effects already have been judged as fearful. And in

123

> overlooking this, is it protected and kept separate from healing. For a miracle is *now*. It stands already here, in present grace, within the only interval of time that sin and fear have overlooked, but which is all there is to time.
>
> The working out of all correction takes no time at all. Yet the acceptance of the working out can seem to take forever. The change of purpose the Holy Spirit brought to your relationship has in it all effects that you will see. They can be looked at *now*. Why wait till they unfold in time and fear they may not come, although already there? You have been told that everything brings good that comes from God. And yet it seems that this is not so. (T-26.VIII.5-6)

We are at a point that the Course refers to in many different ways, for example, "…there is no exception except in the ego's judgment." (T-4.V.1) The script is written. (W-158.4) Everything is in perfect divine order if it is seen and perceived correctly. The choice for right perception is a choice that is available right now, and only right now. The belief that salvation is in the future is the fear of accepting the correction this instant and so projecting it to time:

> Be not content with future happiness. It has no meaning, and is not your just reward. For you have cause for freedom *now*. What profits freedom in a prisoner's form? Why should deliverance be disguised as death? Delay is senseless, and the "reasoning" that would maintain effects of present cause must be delayed until a future time, is merely a denial of the fact that consequence and cause must come as one. Look not to time, but to the little space between you still, to be delivered from. And do not let it be disguised as time, and so preserved because its form is changed and what it *is* cannot be recognized.

The Holy Spirit's purpose now is yours. Should not His happiness be yours as well? (T-26.VIII.9)

The mind is continually prompted by the ego to keep changing the form, to keep looking for salvation, peace and happiness in idols. Whereas with the Course and the Holy Spirit's new purpose there is an emphasis on the meaninglessness of form; it is only by holding to the Holy Spirit's purpose – the one intention that the Holy Spirit offers – that happiness and peace and salvation are ever accepted. The acceptance of this purpose can only take place right now.

## NEW IDEAS ABOUT TIME

David: To close on our topic of time, we look again at Workbook lesson 7 – "I see only the past:"

> Old ideas about time are very difficult to change because everything you believe is rooted in time, and depends on your not learning these new ideas about it. Yet that is precisely why you need new ideas about time. (W-7.2)

We see that the self-concept is based on a time-space belief. The belief in time, as we just read, is an ego concept that is a defense against the holy instant – against the recognition that salvation is now! In the next lesson we see that the deceived mind is preoccupied with past thoughts, with thoughts that have been projected out to form the images on the screen that the deceived mind sees or thinks it sees:

> My mind is preoccupied with past thoughts. This idea is, of course, the reason why you see only the past. No one really sees anything. He sees only his thoughts projected outward. The mind's preoccupation with the past

> is the cause of the misconception about time from which your seeing suffers. Your mind cannot grasp the present, which is the only time there is. It therefore cannot understand time, and cannot, in fact, understand anything. The one wholly true thought one can hold about the past is that it is not here. To think about it at all is therefore to think about illusions. Very few have realized what is actually entailed in picturing the past or in anticipating the future. The mind is actually blank when it does this, because it is not really thinking about anything. (W 8.1-2)

Here we have a clear description of the deception. Mind is preoccupied with past thoughts. These thoughts are projected outward; the images that are seen are therefore images of the past. The mind sees a sequence of events that seem to be happening. It sees itself as if it is a body within the time-space universe when in fact the whole hallucination is basically an old script that is long ago finished. Even the thought which produced that script is completely gone. The holy instant and the real thoughts of the mind are available if the mind can lay aside these projected past thoughts and accept the correction in this instant.

In lesson 181 we take another look at the past and future–time as the ego sees it–as a defense against the acceptance of the correction right now. We will pick it up in the middle of the page:

> We do not care about our future goals. And what we saw an instant previous has no concern for us within this interval of time wherein we practice changing our intent. We seek for innocence and nothing else. We seek for it with no concern but now. A major hazard to success has been involvement with your past and future goals. You have been quite preoccupied with how extremely

different the goals this course is advocating are from those you held before. And you have also been dismayed by the depressing and restricting thought that, even if you should succeed, you will inevitably lose your way again. How could this matter? For the past is gone; the future but imagined. These concerns are but defenses against present change of focus in perception. Nothing more. We lay these pointless limitations by a little while. We do not look to past beliefs, and what we will believe will not intrude upon us now. We enter in the time of practicing with one intent; to look upon the sinlessness within. (W-181.3-5)

This is a very clear statement. The Course offers a metaphysical solution to the perceived problem of the world – this very instant – if we choose to accept it. All of the thoughts, all of the beliefs, all of the processes that we believe we must go through can be circumvented with the acceptance of the correction – the acceptance of the sinlessness within – in this very instant. This is quite an extraordinary idea considering that almost every spiritual path involves the idea of *process*, of trying to reach a future goal of enlightenment. But these passages about time and the power of the present moment offer the opportunity to escape the world of dreaming *in an instant*. Let's close with the first paragraph from lesson 80:

Let me recognize my problems have been solved. If you are willing to recognize your problems, you will recognize that you have no problems. Your one central problem has been answered, and you have no other. Therefore, you must be at peace. Salvation thus depends on recognizing this one problem, and understanding that it has been solved. One problem, one solution. Salvation is accomplished. (W-80.1)

ALSO BY DAVID HOFFMEISTER

Awakening through *A Course in Miracles*
Healing in Mind
Movie Watcher's Guide to Enlightenment
Only One Mind
Purpose is the Only Choice
Quantum Forgiveness
The Mystical Teachings of Jesus
Unwind Your Mind Back to God - Experiencing *A Course in Miracles*

David's writings are available in print and ebook formats.
Select materials have been translated into Chinese, Danish,
Dutch, Finnish, French, German, Hungarian, Japanese,
Norwegian, Portuguese, Spanish, Russian and Swedish.

ONLINE MATERIALS

acim.me — Searchable Audios
acim.biz — ACIM Portal Site
mwge.org — Movie Watcher's Guide to Enlightenment
livingmiracles.org — Living Miracles Central Website
miracleshome.org — Teacher of Teachers
levelsofmind.com — The Fast Track to Peace
awakening-mind.org — Foundation for the Awakening Mind
acim-online-video.net — Searchable Videos
davidhoffmeister.com — About David Hoffmeister and His Teachings
course-in-miracles.com — David Hoffmeister Books and Resources

BIBLIOGRAPHY

*A Course in Miracles*, second ed.
Foundation for Inner Peace,
Mill Valley, CA 1996